W9-ABD-355

*Presented To:*

Jeff & Carrie

*Presented By:*

Paul & June Klotz

Grandpa & Grandma Klotz

*Date:*

June 29th, 2002

# God's Little Devotional Book for Couples

Honor Books
Tulsa, Oklahoma

*God's Little Devotional Book for Couples*
ISBN 1-56292-476-1

P.O. Box 55388
Tulsa, Oklahoma 74155

# God's Little Devotional Book for Couples

# Introduction

There is perhaps no greater joy than sharing "moments of the soul" with a spouse—reading a passage from the Scriptures together or reading to each other words of inspiration that can brighten a day, give encouragement, and cause a smile or tug at the heart.

We encourage you to read these devotionals together as a couple. Perhaps one a day. Perhaps several at a time. Take turns reading to each other. Talk about what is said, if you desire, or let the words speak for themselves.

Take joy in your relationship. Marriage is a relationship of highest value. Keep yours strong, alive, and fresh!

Above all, we encourage you to spend time in prayer together on a daily basis. It is in prayer that hearts are truly knit together as one.

## *The family begins in a commitment of love.*

If you were to hold a lump of dark green clay in one hand, and a lump of light green clay in the other, you could clearly identify the two shades of color. However, if you were to mold the two lumps together, kneading them thoroughly until they were truly blended, you would see just one lump of green clay . . . at least at first glance. Upon closer inspection, you could see the distinct and separate lines of dark and light green clay, yet it would be virtually impossible to separate the clay into two pure colors again.

That is an image of what it means for a husband and wife to become "one flesh"—love binds the couple together, especially as they knead out some of their differences and develop a life of mutual goals, activities, and relationship.

A grandma once told her young granddaughter that Jim and June were coming for a visit. With eager anticipation, they baked special treats and cleaned the house thoroughly in expectation of the couple's overnight stay. With wide-eyed wonder the little girl exclaimed upon their arrival, "Nanna, there are two people. Someone came with Jim-and-June!" When the name of one is so readily associated with the other . . . the clay truly has been blended!

*For this reason a man shall leave his father and his mother and shall be joined to his wife, and the two shall become one flesh.*

EPHESIANS 5:31 AMP

Marriage involves a blending of lives, not merely a "joining." Many marriages flounder because the individuals in them keep looking back over their shoulders at freedoms and relationships they had in the past. When a couple invites Jesus Christ to be the cornerstone of their marriage as the true point of strength on which they build their relationship—they are inviting Him to "walk out front" before them. Then He is free to lead them *forward* into the unique purpose He has for them *as a married couple*.

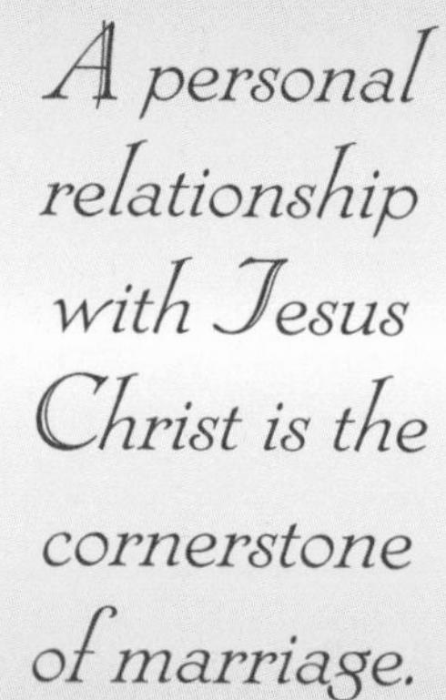

*A personal relationship with Jesus Christ is the cornerstone of marriage.*

We are unique as individuals. But each marriage is also unique. It is as "individual" and one-of-a-kind as the two people involved. Just as God created us as completely original individuals, so we need to invite Him to create our marriages as completely original relationships. This can only happen when each person in the relationship yields his or her individuality to God's higher purpose.

As C. S. Lewis said, "Self exists to be abdicated. In self-giving we touch a rhythm, not only of all creation, but of all being, for the Eternal Word also gives Himself in sacrifice."

*BEHOLD I LAY IN ZION A CHOICE STONE,*
*A PRECIOUS CORNER STONE, AND HE WHO*
*BELIEVES IN HIM WILL NOT BE DISAPPOINTED.*
I PETER 2:6 NAS

# *The most important thing a father can do for his children is to love their mother.*

*Washington Post* columnist William Raspberry wrote a loving tribute to his wife, seemingly unaware that he was reflecting his own role in her success: "The second Sunday in May was not just Mother's Day for our family—it was Mother's Graduation Day, one of the great moments in our household.

"My wife, Sondra, was one of those 'responsible' young women who decided after high school to spare her family the economic burden of college and go directly to work. Then she got married, and her family became her first priority.

"I don't know precisely what made her decide to go back to school. . . . It wasn't easy, studying part-time while managing the lives of a husband and three children. . . .

"On graduation day, it was announced that she had been inducted into both the adult honor society and Phi Beta Kappa. The kids shrieked as though she had won the Nobel Prize for Smart Moms. Some people may have trouble understanding how we could get excited about something as routine as a bachelor's degree. But if you have ever taken up something difficult and made a howling success of it, you'll understand why we are so proud."

*Husbands, love your wives, as Christ loved the church and gave Himself up for her.*

EPHESIANS 5:25 AMP

In their book, *My Lover, My Friend,* Colleen and Louis Evans, Jr. write: "David and Nancy Low are one of the most exciting young couples we have met since coming to Washington. He is a financial lawyer, and she is a top-flight public relations administrator. . . .

"After working in another state for a well-known and respected political leader, Nancy was offered a very high position in a federal government agency. This opportunity was made even more exciting by the fact that it had never before been offered to a woman. David felt the offer was a high honor and urged Nancy to accept it. He was confident he could find a job in his field in Washington. So, submitting

*Love is being willing to face the risks of seeing your spouse's dreams come true.*

to Nancy's career potential, they pulled up stakes and settled here.

"Some men would be threatened by this type of situation. If a man wanted to prove that he didn't need other people, if he were an emotional do-it-yourselfer, then he might resist the emergence of his wife's career, especially if it were an outstanding one. But David is a strong man, eager and able to become a servant to Nancy's development. That is healthy 'headship' and management."

*This is how we know what love is: Jesus Christ laid down his life for us. And we ought to lay down our lives for our brothers.*

I JOHN 3:16 NIV

*Nothing beats love at first sight except love with insight.*

In *One Woman's Liberation,* Shirley Boone writes: "Talk about blind adoration! When Pat and I married, I was so much in love I didn't have any sense at all. Pat has said in interviews that we married fully aware of the serious adjustments we'd have to make and the financial crises we'd face, but he was speaking strictly for himself. As far as I was concerned, I wasn't aware of anything except that he was wonderful and that life without him would be miserable.

"I understood exactly how Mary, Queen of Scots, must have felt when she said of James Bothwell, her third husband, 'I'd follow him to the ends of the earth in my petticoat,' because that's how I felt about Pat.

. . . If Pat had suggested it, I would have gone with him to Timbuktu without batting an eye. He was my life. To me, he was perfect, and that was the beginning of our troubles, because anyone placed on a pinnacle can go in only one direction: down."

Shirley and Pat Boone worked through their differences to create a strong and lasting marriage, but the beginning of their true success as a couple came when they each recognized this cardinal truth: nobody's perfect.

*The beginning of wisdom is this: Get wisdom, and whatever you get, get insight.*

PROVERBS 4:7 RSV

During the course of their twenty-four years of marriage, Tom accumulated a fortune in the natural gas business. But then, in a twenty-four-month period, he saw the fruit of his labors slip away to creditors and foreclosures. Things became so desperate at one point that in order to make the monthly payment on their house, he had to sell his wife Tina's engagement ring. Finally, Tom was forced out of the oil business altogether. He and Tina lost everything they had.

*The measure of a man is not how great his faith is but how great his love is.*

When things looked the worst, Tom landed a promising job in another industry and slowly began to come out of his personal and professional slump. Nearly two years later, while out to dinner, Tina saw in her husband signs of Tom's old exuberance.

When he took his wife's hand in his own and said, "Tina, you are like this diamond—beautiful, exquisite, precious," she thought her heart would burst. "But where did you get the money?" she asked as he put the ring on her finger.

"You haven't known it," Tom confessed, "but for two years I've been giving plasma once a week. I saved all the money I was paid, and last week I sold my hunting gear. The only hunting I want to do from now on is hunt for ways to love you more. You *are* my life."

*Greater love has no man than this, that a man lay down his life for his friends.*
JOHN 15:13 RSV

*Advice to the wife:*
*Be to his virtues very kind.*
*Be to his faults a little blind.*

Buzzards and bees have a major difference in their feeding habits. Buzzards fly overhead searching for dead animals. When they spy a decaying carcass, they swoop down to gorge themselves on it, stripping it to the bare bones. Honey bees, in contrast, only look for sweet nectar. They are very discriminating as they search through the flowers in a garden.

Buzzards produce nothing in their feeding, except fear in those who behold them at work. Honey bees produce honeycombs, dripping with honey, for health and palate benefits to others.

Just as the bees and buzzards always find what they are seeking, so a spouse can generally find what he or she is looking for. If you focus on your partner's faults and mistakes, you'll find them. Your relationship will become one to be avoided, not cherished. On the other hand, if you seek out the goodness in your spouse, you can find that too! And you may be surprised at how sweet your relationship can become.

Unlike buzzards and bees, creatures that cannot choose their own instincts and behavior, we have a choice in what we *choose* to perceive and comment upon. Choose to affirm. Choose virtue.

*[Love] is not easily angered, it keeps no record of wrongs but rejoices with the truth.*

I Corinthians 13:5,6 niv

Australian James H. Jauncey writes in *Talking With the Heart,* "I once married a Norwegian soldier to a Mexican girl. He could speak a little English but no Spanish. She could speak neither English nor Norwegian. How they got together I'll never know. And what might happen in the future as far as communication was concerned, I could not even guess. But if they were in bad shape language-wise, they were in an infinitely better position than many couples I have known who had complete mastery of the English language. My odd bridal couple had successfully gotten over their message of love to each other and they seemed in remarkable rapport. Perhaps communication is easy in

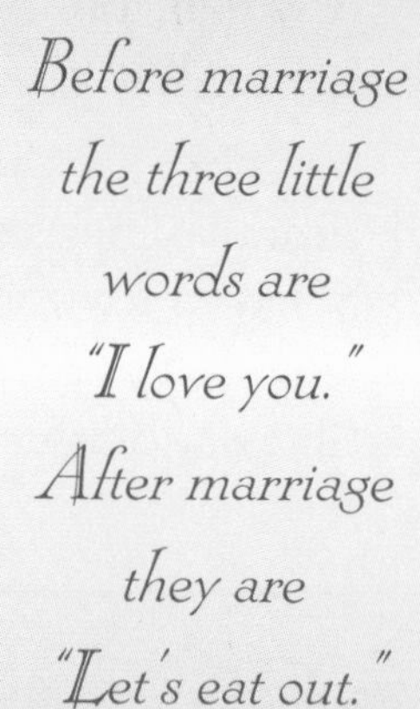

that stage, language or no language. Later on, the emotions have died down and the hidden needs arise. Learning to talk about the needs is a difficult art, and not many learn it."

Romance is the realm of dreams, hopes, and emotions. Marriage, however, is *practical.* It requires a blending of schedules, priorities, chores, obligations. That isn't to say that a marriage cannot include romance—it can . . . and should! But marriage has added dimensions beyond romance, and in that dimension very often lies the "work" of a marriage.

*He that is married careth for*
*the things that are of the world,*
*how he may please* his *wife.*
I CORINTHIANS 7:33 KJV

*A house is made of walls and beams; a home is made of love and dreams.*

A house is just a building. A financial investment. A place that provides shelter.

A home, however, is part of you.

Your fingerprints are on the garden tools. Your children's handprints and footprints may be in the sidewalk cement. Your creativity is painted on the walls and reflected in the fabrics and textures you have chosen. Every step you have ever taken is etched onto your floors.

Your dreams lie just outside your windows. Your ambitions just outside your doors. The tears you have shed have stained your pillows. Little spills and accidents have left their marks too.

Your loved ones are present in silver frames and refrigerator art. Your shelves are lined with the books that have given rise to your thoughts and opinions.

The candle wax on your best linen reminds you of dinner parties, even as your too-large dining room and your silver pieces in the hutch beckon you to entertain again soon. The plants in the garden room are ones of your choosing, ones that have given you joy with each blooming.

A home is always just the right size to hold your memories.

*She looks well to the ways of her household,*
*And does not eat the bread of idleness.*
PROVERBS 31:27 NAS

As Train 8017 made its way through Salerno, Italy, on March 2, 1944, it gave no sign that disaster was in the making. The chugging train didn't collide with anything on that rain-soaked evening. It didn't derail or burn. But shortly after 1:00 A.M., the train loaded with 600 passengers lumbered into the Galleria delle Armi. When the two locomotives pulling the train reached mid-tunnel, its drivewheels began to slip. Sand was sprayed on the tracks but to no avail. The wheels lost traction and the train stopped. All else is speculation since both engineers died. Carbon monoxide snuffed out the lives of nearly 500 people.

*The direction of your thought life can determine the course of your marriage.*

As analysts surveyed the wreckage, they found that the leading locomotive was unbraked, its controls set in reverse. The second locomotive was also unbraked, but its throttle was positioned "full ahead." The two locomotives had pulled and pushed against each other, their engineers obviously having fatally different ideas about what to do! Some have speculated that *no* lives would have been lost if the engineers had only been in agreement about which direction to go.

Make a decision today with your spouse that you will both move your thought life in the direction of God—then stay close by the controls of your minds.

*Keep thy heart with all diligence;*
*for out of it* are *the issues of life.*
PROVERBS 4:23 KJV

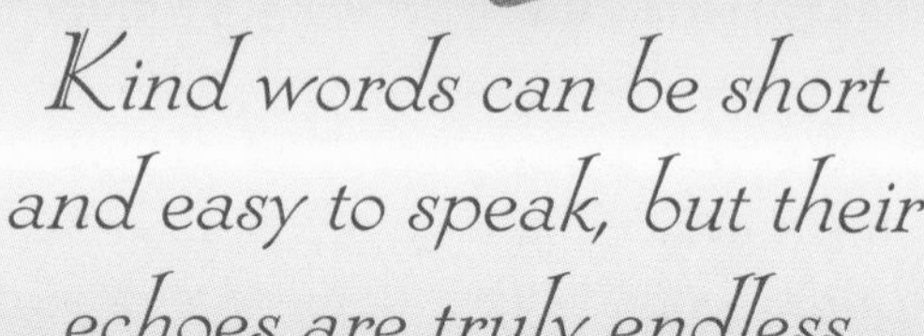

*Kind words can be short and easy to speak, but their echoes are truly endless.*

The words of this poem are a good reminder that what we say can and does make a difference—especially to those whom we love and with whom we live daily:

Is anybody happier
    Because you passed his way?
Does anyone remember
    That you spoke to him today?
This day is almost over,
    And its toiling time is through;
Is there anyone to utter now
    A friendly word for you?
Can you say tonight in passing
    With the days that slipped so fast,

That you helped a single person,
    Of the many that you passed?
Is a single heart rejoicing
    Over what you did or said?
Does one whose hopes were fading
    Now with courage look ahead?
Did you waste the day, or lose it?
    Was it well or poorly spent?
Did you leave a trail of kindness
    Or a scar of discontent?

*Pleasant words* are *as an honeycomb, sweet to the soul, and health to the bones.*
PROVERBS 16:24 KJV

Nathaniel came home heartbroken. How could he tell his wife that he had just been fired from his job at the customhouse? The last thing he wanted her to think was that he was a failure, and yet "failure" is just the label he felt was embroidered on his chest.

*A loving spouse can see the good in you even when you can't.*

To his surprise, when he told his wife what had happened, she responded with joy. "Now you can write your book!" she said optimistically.

"And what shall we live on while I am writing it?" Nathaniel replied with dejection.

His wife Sophia immediately went to a drawer and to his amazement, pulled out a substantial sum of money and handed it to him.

"Where did you get this?" he said in great surprise.

"I have always known you were a man of genius," Sophia said. "I knew that someday you would write a masterpiece. Every week, out of the money you gave me for the housekeeping, I saved a little bit. Here is enough to last us for one whole year."

So Nathaniel Hawthorne, buoyed by his wife's confidence, turned his hand to writing *The Scarlet Letter.*

*Be patient with each other, making allowance for each other's faults because of your love.*
EPHESIANS 4:2 TLB

*Children have more need of models than of critics.*

When Dr. F. W. Norwood was a minister in Australia, he approached a man about joining the church. The man immediately and brusquely refused. Norwood said, "I did not get on my knees to the man to plead with him to join the church. I wouldn't do that to any man."

But to Norwood's surprise, the man came forward after a church service a few months later and asked to be made a member. Dr. Norwood asked him after the service what had caused his change of heart. The man replied, "You know I have a little boy. A week or so ago I was taking him for a walk in the country when we came to a rather rugged pathway where we had to walk in single file. I was going on ahead, and had forgotten the lad was finding the way a little more difficult than myself. Suddenly I heard his small voice say, 'Be careful where you step, daddy, I'm coming on behind!' That settled it, sir. I want to join the church."

In so many ways, you represent Christ to your children. It is through your eyes that they come to see Him and love Him. It is through you that they learn the meaning of the word—Christian.

*Be their ideal; let them follow the way you teach and live; be a pattern for them in your love, your faith, and your clean thoughts.*

I TIMOTHY 4:12 TLB

Author Charlie W. Shedd shares "Our Seven Official Rules for a Good, Clean Fight" in the book he wrote to his daughter, *Letters to Karen:*

1. Before we begin we must both agree that the time is right.
2. We will remember that our only aim is deeper understanding.
3. We will check our weapons often to be sure they're not deadly.
4. We will lower our voices one notch instead of raising them two.
5. We will never quarrel or reveal private matters in public.

*An argument is the longest distance between two points.*

6. We will discuss an armistice whenever either of us calls "halt."
7. When we have come to terms, we will put it away till we both agree it needs more discussing.

Says Shedd, "No small part of the zest in a good marriage comes from working through differences. Learning to zig and zag with the entanglements; studying each other's reactions under pressure; handling one another's emotions intelligently—all these offer a challenge that simply can't be beat for sheer fun and excitement."

*When angry, do not sin; do not ever let your wrath (your exasperation, your fury or indignation) last until the sun goes down.*
EPHESIANS 4:26 AMP

*It is our uniqueness that gives freshness and vitality to a relationship.*

Mark and Joanne were not only married, but they shared a clinical practice as dentists. To the outsider, Mark and Joanne seemed like complete opposites, which they readily admitted they were.

"We're different in virtually every way," Joanne admits. "Mark can't balance a checkbook, but I'm good at accounting. He is great at dealing with the salesmen who come in to the clinic; I tend to buy too much of everything they show me. I'm much neater than he is, but he doesn't bring home problems the way I do. When we got out of dental school, we were advised *never* to go into partnership with each other."

"For awhile," Mark added, "we took that advice. Then I realized that I was bringing my books home for Joanne to balance and she was asking me to cancel orders from salesmen. So we decided that rather than deny our differences, we'd use them!"

Mark and Joanne sought a professional counselor who could advise them how to make their differences work *for* them rather than against them, and at the same time, not promote their common weaknesses into codependency.

"We're unique," they conclude. "But we're also a team. If we were identical, we'd probably be bored."

*I am fearfully* and *wonderfully made.*
PSALM 139:14 KJV

In *Love for a Lifetime,* Dr. James Dobson writes: "I'll never forget the time a few years ago when our daughter had just learned to drive . . . Shirley and I covenanted between us to pray for our son and daughter at the close of every day. Not only were we concerned about the risk of an automobile accident, but we were also aware of so many other dangers that lurk out there in a city like Los Angeles."

*Give your troubles to God; He will be up all night anyway.*

One night the Dobsons were particularly tired and collapsed into bed without their benedictory prayer. They were almost asleep when they remembered to pray for their children's safety. Later they learned that their daughter Danae and a girlfriend had gone to a fast-food establishment to buy hamburgers and cokes. They had then driven up the road a few miles and were sitting in the car eating their meal when a policeman drove by, shining his spotlight in al directions. Moments after he moved on, Danae and her friend heard a "clunk" from under the car. Within seconds, a man crawled out from under their car and emerged on the passenger side! Danae quickly started the car and sped safely away.

Shirley and James Dobson realized they had been on their knees at the precise moment of danger.

*Casting all your anxiety upon Him,*
*because He cares for you.*
I PETER 5:7 NAS

# *Our prayer life never needs a bridle, but sometimes it needs a spur.*

A boy was watching a holy man praying on the banks of a river. When he had completed his prayer, the boy went over and asked him, "Will you teach me to pray?"

The man studied the boy's face carefully. Then he gripped the boy's head in his hands, and plunged it forcefully into the water! The boy struggled frantically, trying to free himself to breathe. When the man finally released his hold, the little boy gasped for breath, then asked, "What did you do that for?"

The holy man said, "I just gave you your first lesson."

The boy asked, "What do you mean?"

The holy man replied, "When you long to pray as much as you wanted to breathe, only then will I be able to teach you to pray."

We are wise to pray about small matters in our marriages and not hold our prayers only for times of crisis or when we face major challenges. Indeed, if we are in the habit of praying about the small problems we encounter, major problems may never arise!

*Is any one of you in trouble?*
*He should pray.*
JAMES 5:13 NIV

Columnist Erma Bombeck has written: "At some point in your life—if you are lucky—you throw practicality to the wind and start living.

*Men for the sake of getting a living forget to live.*

"A lot of things can bring about your rebirth. With me, it was a case of the evening news. I was sitting around one night flipping between Dan, Peter, and Tom, who were giving me my state-of-the-world fix. After hearing about drugs, crime, bad air, tainted fish, holes in the atmosphere, cyanide-laced fruits, and people blowing each other up, I said aloud, 'That tears it. Life is too short to eat brown bananas.'

"I know that's a strange metaphor, but it sort of sums up my life. Every week, I buy fresh bananas, but I can't eat them until I've eaten up the semi-rotten ones from the week before. By the time they are gone, the fresh ones are getting rotten. . . .

"I took a long, hard look at my sensible life and began to question it . . . Our generation sometimes criticizes 'baby boomers' priorities: a cappuccino maker today, next year a steam iron. But maybe baby boomers know something.

"This week I bought the prettiest bananas I could find. I'm in control. I'll eat them when I say they're ready to be eaten."

*"So don't worry at all about having enough food and clothing. Why be like the heathen? For they take pride in all these things and are deeply concerned about them. But your heavenly Father already knows perfectly well that you need them."*

MATTHEW 6:31 TLB

# *The best way to hold a man is in your arms.*

Our ability to become emotionally involved with others and to be vulnerable to them is directly related to our experiences of having been stroked, caressed, and cuddled as children. We learn affection from the tender models in our lives. We learn from the warmth of being held close.

Before birth, a baby is enveloped in the soft, warm embrace of the womb. After birth, the child left untouched and uncuddled will form a bond with anything given it to touch, even a stuffed toy. If all human tactile experience is denied, the baby will die.

Our need for touch continues throughout our lifetime. In fact, our body chemistry changes when we are physically close to another person. When a person is touched, the amount of hemoglobin in the blood—which carries oxygen and helps prevent disease and speed recovery from illness—increases significantly. In one animal study, rabbits that were held close and stroked often developed less hardening of the arteries than unstroked, unhugged rabbits!

If you are uncomfortable with intimacy or close contact, you can *learn* to become comfortable. It will require effort, but the results will be worth it!

*May your unfailing love be my comfort,*
*according to your promise to your servant.*
PSALM 119:76 NIV

Groaning as he helped his wife wash the dishes one evening, the Reverend John Byrnell protested, "This isn't a man's job!"

His wife immediately wiped her hands and reached for the family Bible on the nearby dining table. "Oh yes it is," she said as she turned to 2 Kings 21:13 and read aloud to her husband, "I will wipe Jerusalem as a man wipeth a dish, wiping it, and turning it upside down."

*The best way for you and your spouse to guarantee some time without the kids is to do the dinner dishes together.*

Doing things together is at the core of marriage. You may not feel led or be able to do what one married couple—both ordained Presbyterian ministers—did in Bellevue, Washington, but their example is certainly one of a shared life:

- They joined their names with a hyphen, each using the full hyphenated name.
- They shared one ministerial position as "associate pastor."
- Each was on the job half the time and each received half the pay.
- Each did half the household work.

Time together is something you likely will need to *schedule* in your marriage. Why not phone and make an appointment with your spouse? Call it a date!

*Two can accomplish more than twice as much as one, for the results can be much better.*
ECCLESIASTES 4:9 TLB

*What is a home without a Bible? 'Tis a home where daily bread for the body is provided, but the soul is never fed.*

Leonard E. LeSourd has written about his late wife, Catherine Marshall, the author of *Christy:* "Bibles were scattered throughout our house . . . all editions, plus reference books and concordances. We often went to bed, turned out the light, and listened to a chapter of scripture on tape. If she could have found a way to spread Bible passages on a slice of bread, Catherine would have devoured it.

"When upset or under spiritual assault or in physical pain, Catherine would go to her office, kneel by her chair, and open her Bible. . . . She would read, then pray, then read, then pray some more. She liked to pray with the Bible clutched in her hands. . . . She would rest her case on its promises. Catherine didn't read the Bible for solace or inspiration, but to have an encounter with the Lord. . . . I think these were the most intense moments of her life. . . . Catherine's passion for the Word permeated her whole life. It undergirded her writing. It formed a base for us as a married team in the making of family decisions. It provided substance to her counseling of people through the mail. I'm convinced it was also the basis for her inner vitality, her charisma, and the mantle of authority she wore with some reluctance."

*"It is written, 'Man shall not live*
*by bread alone, but by every word*
*that proceeds from the mouth of God.'"*
MATTHEW 4:4 RSV

A child once asked his father to draw a picture of a stepladder for him. The father did as he was asked. Then his son said, "No, Dad, you left out something."

*The closer a man and his wife get to Christ, the clearer they see how important it is for them to stay close to each other.*

The father looked again at the double upside-down V he had drawn on the page and the lines he had drawn as the ladder's steps. "What did I leave out?" he asked.

The little boy replied, "The part where you put the paint can."

The little boy may have been more interested in paint cans than a properly engineered ladder. But what the father later realized was that the "crosspiece" that extends to provide a resting place for paint cans is the one part of a stepladder that is truly indispensable! Without it, the inverted V shape of a ladder would collapse to the ground. It is the crosspiece that allows a stepladder to support weight in order to be useful.

If a couple is only joined by a recited vow, their marriage may quickly collapse. If Christ, however, forms the crosspiece that holds their lives into a sturdy triangular shape, they can withstand much pressure.

*Though a man might prevail against one who is alone, two will withstand him. A threefold cord is not quickly broken.*
ECCLESIASTES 4:12 RSV

*Children are natural mimics—they act like their parents in spite of every attempt to teach them good manners.*

Author Ken Anderson tells of a time when he and his wife took their large family to visit Ashland Manor, the home of Henry Clay. A docent followed the family through several rooms and then returned to her desk in the lobby. As the family prepared to leave, she said, "I must tell you something. Never in my life have I seen such a large group of well-mannered children."

One of the Anderson children then piped up, "Boy, Dad, it's a good thing she doesn't see us sometimes!" Although the family had a good laugh, from that day on the mention of "Ashland manners" brought the children to their best behavior.

The manners children exhibit in public aren't learned there. They are learned at home. When he was president of Princeton University, Woodrow Wilson once told a parents' group: "I get many letters from you parents about your children. You want to know why we people up here in Princeton can't make more out of them and do more for them. . . . The reason is that they are your sons. . . . They have absorbed the ideals of your homes. You have formed and fashioned them. They are your sons. In those malleable, moldable years of their lives, you have forever left your imprint upon them."

*"I have set you an example that you should do as I have done for you."*
JOHN 13:15 NIV

Even though he was single, at age thirty-two Bill decided it was time to buy a house. He found a modestly priced four-bedroom home and began to visualize how he could use the rooms. A few months later, however, he found himself engaged to marry a woman who had three young daughters. Two years after their marriage, Bill and his wife, Dee, had a baby. The gym and TV room he had envisioned in his new home never materialized!

*Love makes a house a home.*

It took Bill and Dee four jobs to pay for the life they had chosen, but although their schedules were relentless, Bill couldn't help but conclude, "Ain't life grand?" Eventually, his stepdaughters began to leave home and Bill once again made plans for the spare rooms in the house. But his elderly parents needed help, and Bill and Dee invited them to move in. Even in getting up at night to help his ailing father, Bill still was of the opinion, "Ain't life grand?"

After more than twenty-five years, Bill still doesn't have his "dream house." What he has had, however, is two decades of a real *home.*

*You will be happy and it will be well with you.*
*Your wife shall be like a fruitful vine,*
*Within your house,*
*Your children like olive plants*
*Around your table.*
PSALMS 128:2-3 NAS

*You will never "find" time for anything. If you want time, you must make it.*

Colleen Evans writes in *My Lover, My Friend:* "I'm not sure exactly what I said, but between sniffs and sobs . . . I told him how hungry I was to be with him, to have time to talk and dream, alone. I shared my strong feeling that there had to be a change in our relentless schedule, a change that would give us time to communicate and build our relationship. . . .

"We sat and talked for a very long time, saying things we both wanted and needed to hear . . . I remember Louie thanked me for being honest about my feelings. . . . And then he did a simple, practical—and, to me, very beautiful—thing. He took his little date book from his pocket, and looked until he found a free night. It happened to be Thursday of the following week, and he said, 'That's our night'. . . . Out of that night came a decision to put aside time every week for the same purpose . . . and so it has been in all the years since . . . Thursday night.

"Now I'm sure many couples are able to *find* time for each other in an easy, unscheduled way, and that's wonderful. But that didn't work for us. With our kind of life we found we had to *make* time."

*Whatever your hand finds to do,*
*do it with all your might.*
ECCLESIASTES 9:10 NIV

Two men once made small talk at a party: "You and your wife seem to get along very well," one man said. "Don't you ever have differences?"

"Sure," said the other. "We often have differences, but we get over them quickly."

"How do you do that?" the first man asked.

"Simple," said the second, "I don't tell her we have them."

*The kind of music people should have in their homes is domestic harmony.*

In *Letters to Philip,* Charles Shedd describes a slightly different situation—harmony that comes after love has conquered conflict. He writes: "In one town where I lived two rivers met. There was a bluff high above them where you could sit and watch their coming together. . . . Those two nice streams came at each other like fury. I have actually seen them on days when it was almost frightening to watch. They clashed in a wild commotion of frenzy and confusion. . . . Then, as you watched, you could almost see the angry white caps pair off, bow in respect to each other, and join forces as if to say, 'Let us get along now. Ahead of us there is something better.' Sure enough, on downstream, at some distance, the river swept steadily on once more."

*And above all these put on love, which binds everything together in perfect harmony.*

COLOSSIANS 3:14 RSV

*Ninety percent of the friction of daily life is caused by the wrong tone of voice.*

In *Listening for God's Silent Language,* Don Osgood writes: "We stood in our kitchen that morning looking at each other, caught by some force. . . . We were facing each other across the small floor space between the kitchen sink and the refrigerator, but really across the wide divide of my focus on success in a new business and Joan's focus on a new set of ideas fostered by a seminary.

"'So . . . that's the path for you, is it?' 'It is.'

"'Then maybe you should follow your own path and I'll follow mine.' 'Maybe so.' 'Maybe we should sell the house, split the equity, and walk our separate ways until things settle down.'

"It was a tense moment. A moment for growth in our marriage or for irreplaceable loss. We had groped our way to the edge of a cliff, we were standing on the point of no return.

"No. . . . We don't need to sell our house to work things out. We can stay right here. We've been together a long time. Maybe we can learn how to get through this.' It was a huge moment, stepping back from the crumbling edge. Nothing was really settled—all our disagreements still hung out there in the air. And yet somehow everything was changed—inside."

*A man finds joy in giving an apt reply—*
*and how good is a timely word!*
PROVERBS 15:23 NIV

Although Kim wasn't a great cook, she decided to try to make something "from scratch" for the church potluck. On the way to the event, both she and her husband Hank could smell the charred aroma of a sauce that had been scorched before it was added to her casserole.

*Marriage must exemplify friendship's highest ideal, or else it will be a failure.*

When they arrived at the potluck, Kim's casserole was placed on the table along with the other food dishes. Before anyone came to the table, Kim spooned a bit of the casserole out for Hank to taste it. The look on his face confirmed her worst nightmare. *What would her new friends think of her now?*

Before anyone else came to the table, Hank picked up Kim's casserole and announced to the group that he was going to make a pig out of himself and eat Kim's casserole all by himself. He noted that there were plenty of other hot dishes, salads, and desserts for the rest of them—but after all, he asked, how often did he get his favorite dish?

Hank sat in a corner courageously eating most of the "casserole for four" before anyone else could taste it. And though they laughed about it later, Kim told her friends for years, "I knew then I had married a man I would do my best to keep forever."

*"And here is how to measure it—*
*the greatest love is shown when a*
*person lays down his life for his friends."*
JOHN 15:13 TLB

*A wise lover values not so much the gift of the lover as the love of the giver.*

The ability to give is, in itself, a gift—a manifestation of God's goodness to a person. If you have trouble giving, ask God to give you a spirit of generosity and a willingness to give!

George MacDonald writes in *The Word of Jesus on Prayer,* "For the real good of every gift it is essential, first, that the giver be in the gift—as God always is, for He is love—and next, that the receiver know and receive the giver in the gift. Every gift of God is but a harbinger of His greatest and only sufficing gift—that of Himself. No gift unrecognized as coming from God is at its own best: therefore many things that God would gladly give us must wait until we ask for them, that we may know whence they come. When in all gifts we find Him, then in Him we shall find all things."

Choose your gifts wisely. Put yourself into them—your time, your creativity, your sensitivity to the other person's needs and desires.

When you receive a gift, look beyond its surface appearance and value to see the one who gave it. Receive the giver's "present" as an act of their love and desire to have a relationship with you.

*How fair is thy love, my sister,* my *spouse! how much better is thy love than wine! and the smell of thine ointments than all spices!*
SONG OF SOLOMON 4:10 KJV

Elizabeth endured hell on earth during her formative years. She was one of eleven children born to a father who was an oppressive, dictatorial tyrant. His angry rages often sent sensitive Elizabeth to her bed with any variety of ills.

*There is no more lovely, friendly and charming relationship, communion or company than a good marriage.*

It wasn't until she was forty years old that Elizabeth met Robert. Robert did not see her as a sickly middle-aged invalid. Rather, he saw her as a beautiful, talented woman just waiting to blossom. He loved her with all his heart and withstood several brutal confrontations with Elizabeth's controlling father before he finally won her hand in marriage.

Glowing in love for each other, they traveled the European continent, marveling at God's wonders and at their own love. At forty-three, Elizabeth gave birth to a healthy baby. Their lives were full and beautiful. In great joy, Elizabeth wrote to her husband the incomparable words of "How Do I Love Thee?"—perhaps the best known of her *Sonnets From the Portuguese.* True loveliness and charm had wonderfully entered Elizabeth Barrett's life when she became Elizabeth Barrett Browning.

*A wife of noble character*
*is her husband's crown.*
PROVERBS 12:4 NIV

*You can do everything else right as a parent, but if you don't begin with loving God, you're going to fail.*

In *Fit to Be Tied,* Bill and Lynne Hybels write: "There is a cruel, ungodly world out there that wants to eat our kids for lunch. Our son was offered drugs when he was ten years old and taunted by friends to 'have sex' with a fourth grade girl. In the halls of her suburban high school our daughter is daily bombarded with profanity and sexual innuendoes, with immoral lifestyles and alluring temptations. Never before have our children and yours so needed the advantage of being led by parents with shared values and beliefs; there is power in a unified front. But you can't fake that. Kids pick up on the discrepancies. So, what do they do when they sense that the two primary authority figures in their lives don't agree on the basics? What do they believe? What do they have to go on? What can they grab on to and say, 'This must be true?' How can they determine right from wrong?

"The only way to present a united front is to marry someone who has the same Lord—someone who cherishes the same treasure, trusts the same blueprint, and taps the same strength. Only then can you share the same values and establish a home where children can get the kind of guidance they need."

*But as for me and my house,*
*we will serve the LORD.*
JOSHUA 24:15 RSV

After he had been in the ministry for several years, a pastor was preparing a special sermon on love. When he went to his file cabinet to pull out the "Love" file of material he had collected through the years, he was shocked to find that he didn't have such a file!

*A happy marriage is the union of two good forgivers.*

Thinking this to be virtually impossible, since he knew he had collected many anecdotes and quotes about love, he began searching through the cabinet folder by folder. He fully expected to find the Love folder stuck in another folder. He searched among the folders on Faith and Fasting, Healing and Heaven, even Christology and Christian Education. But he didn't have one on Love.

As he sat and pondered this situation, he began to think back over the sermons he had preached over the years. Then he suddenly realized that he had used bits and pieces of Love material in preparing dozens of other sermons. Quickly he went back to the cabinet, and sure enough, he found parts of the Love file in the folders labeled Patience, Kindness, Humility, Trust, Hope, Loyalty, and Perseverance. The greatest amount of material on love, however, was found in his file labeled Forgiveness.

*Be kind to one another, tenderhearted,*
*forgiving one another, even*
*as God in Christ forgave you.*
EPHESIANS 4:32 NKJV

*Forgiveness is giving love when there is no reason to. . . .*

When God forgives, something decisive happens. When we forgive, something decisive also happens. In *Healing Life's Hurts,* Matthew and Dennis Linn tell of an inner-healing workshop they observed. The men and women present were all once divorced and had remarried. They had come to the retreat hoping for healing of the anger and hostility they felt toward their former spouses. During the weekend sessions, the remarried couples were slowly and prayerfully led into ways in which they could grow from their past relationships and use what they learned to build new patterns in their current marriages.

After a year, the group gathered to discuss what had happened in the aftermath of the retreat. The Linns reported: "Out of the seven who forgave a former spouse after years of resentment, five found that their former spouses had suddenly made an effort to forgive and build a bridge toward them. One suddenly called a week after the workshop, another traveled two thousand miles to see his family, and another wrote his first letter in ten silent years."

Forgiveness frees a person in the spiritual realm to respond to love, and in experiencing love, one is much more likely to express it!

*"Blessed* are *the merciful,*
*For they shall obtain mercy."*
MATTHEW 5:7 NKJV

Part of our role as family members is to be a "fan" of those with whom we live. We are to be the number-one cheerleader for our spouse and children. In return we receive the knowledge that our children and spouse are hoping we will succeed in every area of our own life.

*We should seize every opportunity to give encouragement. Encouragement is oxygen to the soul.*

E-N-C-O-U-R-A-G-E-M-E-N-T is perhaps the best cheer you can learn!

E is for enthusiasm and energy in supporting causes important to your family members.

N is for saying, "Next time you'll succeed."

C is for compassion.

O is for open lines of communication.

U is for understanding.

R is for rooting on the team.

A is for arranging your schedule to make time for others in your family.

G is for going the second mile.

E is for entertaining your children's friends.

M is for modeling a positive attitude.

E is for empowering your child with God's Word.

N is for never giving up.

T is for taking time out for hugs and praise.

*But encourage one another daily, as long as it is called Today.*

HEBREWS 3:13 NIV

*You can create an oasis of love in the midst of a harsh and uncaring world by grinding it out and sticking in there.*

A loving relationship can provide the nurture necessary to withstand the world's hub-bub, troubles, and pain. In *Quiet Thoughts,* Paul McElroy writes: "There are times when a man cares for nothing but the cessation of his pain. It sometimes seems as if his pain were carried to an extreme and unendurable limit. He turns from it in horror, regards it as useless, and even accuses God of cruelty because the suffering is so intense.

*When sickness comes and bids us rest awhile*
*In some calm pool, beside life's too swift stream,*
*Why rail at Fate, and count ourselves ill used?*

*'Tis then one's soul awakes, weaves dream on dream.*

"Those who have reached the depths claim suffering can be one of the most wonderful experiences of life. It can make us or break us—depending upon how we take it. We can make of it a beacon to light the world and give strength to posterity. Through example, we can demonstrate to others the nobility of a disciplined and undefeated courage. Can we not trust that somehow good will be the final outcome of evil?"

Make your marriage a place where dreams flourish, strength is imparted, and goodness reigns.

*"A new command I give you:*
*Love one another. As I have loved you,*
*so you must love one another."*
JOHN 13:34 NIV

Shortly after Bill and Gail were married, they saw a theater production. Gail thought the leading man was extremely attractive, but Bill disagreed. "It wasn't his physical appearance," Gail said. "He was kind and sensitive, strong in an inner way. That's what I find attractive in a man. Though you don't always act that way, I know you are strong and self-confident on the inside. I love you for that."

*My most brilliant achievement was to be able to persuade my wife to marry me.*

Bill was stunned. He saw himself as anything but self-confident and strong. Usually he let others have their way—to the point where he even let others push him around. So he said, "I thought about what Gail said and decided, I *do* have those qualities and I ought to show them." The next day Bill had a confrontation at work. Although he was nervous, he stood his ground. And with Gail cheering him on, he was soon demonstrating his quiet strength at home and in the community too.

Years later, Bill said, "Gail saw something in me that I hadn't seen in myself. I became someone I never would have become without her support and encouragement."

*To every* thing there is *a season,*
*A time to get.*
ECCLESIASTES 3:1,6 KJV

*The bonds of matrimony are worthless unless the interest is kept up.*

A magnet has two poles. If it doesn't, it isn't a magnet! It's only a useless hunk of scrap iron.

One of the greatest danger signals in a marriage is when either partner no longer feels attracted to the other. This attraction actually has very little to do with youth or sex appeal, as some might think. Attraction is based on how we define and perceive "beauty"—which is an inner quality, not merely a cosmetic or superficial state of prettiness or style. True beauty lies in the image of God. When we see another person as being created in God's image, we begin to see more and more facets of their being and to appreciate more and more of their beauty.

The more we acknowledge the beauty of their creation, the more we are attracted to their beauty.

Part of keeping the magnet working in marriage is seeing your spouse as "God's creation in process." Your spouse may be *influenced* and *encouraged* by you, but ultimately your spouse is God's creation. Your spouse's beauty is rooted in what God is doing in his or her life. The good news—you are privileged to watch your spouse's beauty unfold and to enjoy the person your spouse is becoming!

*Live happily with the woman you love through the fleeting days of life, for the wife God gives you is your best reward down here for all your earthly toil.*

ECCLESIASTES 9:9 TLB

One might not think of a bank's monthly newsletter as the place to read about the importance of good manners in marriage. But consider these wise words a staff member at the Royal Bank of Canada once wrote:

"Many of the things that disturb family life are the product of original mistakes compounded by bad manners. Walter Hines Page, distinguished United States ambassador to Great Britain, said: 'The more I find out about diplomatic customs, and the more I hear of the little-big troubles of others, the more need I find to be careful about details of courtesy.'

*Marriage may be inspired by music, soft words, and perfume, but its security is manifest in work, consideration, respect, and well-fried bacon.*

"If love is the foundation of happy marriage, good manners are the walls and diplomacy is the roof.

"Manners for two are fixed by the same rules as are manners for the million, based upon the Golden Rule. They spring from kindness, courtesy, and consideration, with a dash of *savoir faire*—the faculty of knowing just what to do and how to do it."

For some, the secret of a happy marriage lies in finding out what pleases the other person, then does those pleasing things. For others, the secret lies in discovering what irritates, annoys, or angers another person, then not doing those things!

*Nevertheless let each one of you in particular so love his own wife as himself, and let the wife* see *that she respects* her *husband.*
EPHESIANS 5:33 NKJV

*Many parents are finding out that a pat on the back helps develop character—if given often enough, early enough, and low enough.*

On Halloween night in the year 1900, a ten-year-old boy in Abilene, Kansas, was so angry his face turned crimson. His older brothers were heading out to go trick-or-treating, but he had to stay home. "You're too young to go out," his father told him. The boy burst into tears, ran into the yard, and began punching the trunk of an apple tree.

He later wrote, "My dad suddenly had me by the collar and I was getting a tanning." Then he was sent to bed. As he lay sobbing in his room, his mother came in and offered this advice from the Bible: "He that ruleth his spirit is better than he that taketh a city." (See Proverbs 16:32.) These words, coupled with the spanking, stuck with the young boy. In fact, as he recalled them as a seventy-six-year-old man, President Dwight Eisenhower wrote in his memoirs, "I have always looked back on that conversation as one of the most valuable moments in my life."

A spanking should be more than punishment—it should be a lesson in behavior that your children understand clearly. Make sure your children know why you are spanking them, and what it is that you desire for them to learn from your action.

*Correct your son, and he will give you rest;*
*Yes, he will give delight to your soul.*
PROVERBS 29:17 NKJV

Ann and Paul were intelligent, attractive, warm human beings. Married twenty years, they had four children. On the surface, their lives appeared successful. But inside, things were sour. They both worked at demanding jobs and had little time for each other. As communication faltered, they began to confide in friends, who soon became more serious interests. As the couple considered divorce, they sought out a Christian counselor in the hopes that he might help them make the painful journey of rediscovering each other.

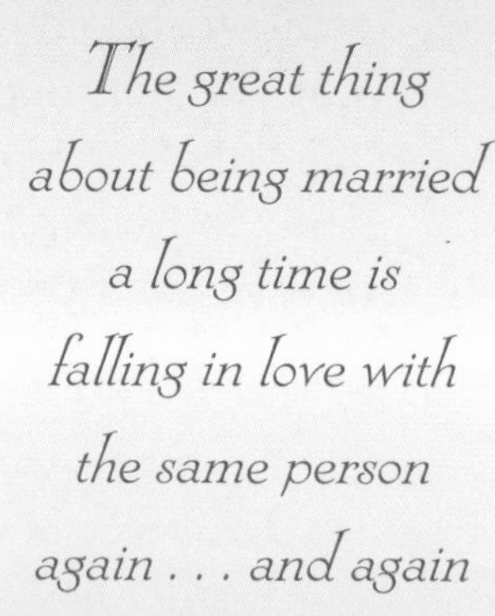


The counselor encouraged each of them to take their hurts to the Lord, the only One who could truly forgive them and heal them, and to pray together. Prayer was a risk for them—*What if it didn't work?* Still, they were willing to try. Over time, their hearts grew softer. A new love was born, and their minister led them in a reuniting service. With their children present, they rededicated their lives to Christ and to each other . . . there wasn't a dry eye in the house.

Not every couple may need such a service, but every marriage needs reuniting in some way every day.

*Let thy fountain be blessed: and rejoice*
*with the wife of thy youth and be*
*thou ravished always with her love.*
PROVERBS 5:18,19 KJV

*To keep your marriage brimming with love in the loving cup, whenever you're wrong, admit it, whenever you're right, shut up.*

Marie Louise de La Ramee says in *Ouida*, "There are many moments in friendship, as in love, when silence is beyond words. The faults of our friend may be clear to us, but it is well to seem to shut our eyes to them.

"Friendship is usually treated by the majority of mankind as a tough and everlasting thing which will survive all manner of bad treatment. But this is an exceedingly great and foolish error, it may die in an hour of a single unwise word."

If "I love you" is the most important three-word phrase in a marriage, "I'm sorry" is probably the most important two-word phrase! The more a spouse is willing to admit fault, the greater the likelihood the other spouse will also grow to be vulnerable enough to admit error. This is not to say that a person should apologize for error that has *not* been made; to do so would be to become a doormat or to manifest a false humility. When one is standing in the right, although the other cannot see it, the better approach is the no-word statement of silence!

*Confess to one another therefore your faults and pray [also] for one another, that you may be healed* and *restored.*
JAMES 5:16 AMP

In *Rock-Solid Marriage,* Robert and Rosemary Barnes write: "Last summer we went with a close friend to his ranch in Jackson Hole, Wyoming. At our friend Gary's insistence, we spent one whole day climbing the side of a mountain to get to see something he wanted us to see. We were both just exhausted, and it got to the point that we really didn't care what was in that special valley. It couldn't be worth all that pain we were going through. He just kept insisting. 'Trust me,' he kept saying, 'you'll be glad you did this when we get there.'

> *A marriage may be made in heaven, but the maintenance must be done on earth.*

"Three hours later, when our feet were blistered and we were dying of thirst, we finally reached our destination. Lying down on a side of a mountain, we were looking at the most beautiful valley and lake I had ever seen. The climb was long and it was agony, but it was more than worth it. Gary was right.

"In the beginning, God established marriage. It wasn't meant to be easy; nothing worth having is. It was meant to be fulfilling and completing. It takes work, but it's almost as if God is saying, 'Trust Me, it's worth the effort!'"

*Practice what you have learned and*
*received and heard and seen in me,*
and *model your way of living on it,*
*and the God of peace (of untroubled,*
*undisturbed well-being) will be with you.*
PHILIPPIANS 4:9 AMP

*The most impressive example of tolerance is a golden wedding anniversary.*

Virginia sat silently as her husband of forty years, Frank, launched into a round of silly camp songs with the children and teens in their living room. The kids loved his enthusiastic singing, and he soon had them singing in rounds and tramping around the room while the adults made their way into quieter areas for more serious conversation.

One of Virginia's friends noticed that Virginia moved to freshen the buffet table as the songfest became more rowdy, then watched her retreat into the kitchen. The friend followed her and said, "Isn't Frank fun? What a sense of humor!"

Virginia just smiled and said, "Actually, I hate those songs and it bothers me when my otherwise very dignified husband acts so silly." Then she quickly added, "But, I've never told Frank that and I never will. He's having a good time, and that's what parties are all about. For that matter, I suspect he doesn't like my fussing so much about the food during a party—but he's never told me so. I guess you could say we give each other enough space to be ourselves."

Tolerance means letting others live uncriticized as they manifest all of their human foibles and personality quirks.

*Let your fountain [of human life]*
*be blessed [with the reward of fidelity],*
*and rejoice in the wife of your youth.*
PROVERBS 5:18 AMP

Martin Luther wrote, "Along comes the clever harlot, namely natural reason, who looks at married life, turns up her nose and says: 'Why, must I rock the baby, wash its diapers, change its bed, smell its odor, heal its rash, take care of this and take care of that, do this, and do that? It is better to remain single and live a quiet and carefree life. I will become a priest or a nun and tell my children to do the same.'

*The best things to get out of marriage are children.*

"But what does the Christian faith say? The father opens his eyes, looks at these lowly, distasteful, and despised things and knows that they are adorned with divine approval as with the most precious gold and silver. God, with His angels and creatures, will smile—not because diapers are washed, but because it is done in faith."

Throughout the Holy Scriptures, children are regarded as a blessing. Most parents would agree with that teaching, although some require years to come to such a conclusion. A research study was conducted several years ago involving women who had once seriously considered aborting a baby. Those women—whose children are now ages four and five—reported their child was loved greatly, and greatly valued!

*Behold, children are a gift of the LORD;*
*The fruit of the womb is a reward.*
PSALM 127:3 NAS

# *First secure an independent income, then practice virtue.*

All of their lives Mary and Walt worked hard. One would have thought they'd be ready to relax when they hit retirement years. They had good health, sufficient income, a home and cars that were paid for and children who were happily married and self-sufficient. "You ought to travel some," their friends advised them. But Mary's response was always, "What would our old friends do?"

By "old friends," Mary was referring to several elderly neighbors who lived nearby. Mary was in the habit of getting up at five in the morning and making her rounds with these neighbors—helping them with their showers and breakfasts. Then she and Walt would return in the afternoon to help them with laundry, housework, and grocery shopping. In the evenings, Mary would bake bread and make casseroles to take to her neighbors. "Old people need someone to help them so they can stay in their own homes," Mary would tell her concerned friends. "Mother always said to me, 'Go see if Mrs. So-and-so needs anything.' And that's still what I'm doing! I'd feel bad if something happened to one of these old people because I failed to help them."

"But Mary," her friend protested, "Your 'old' people are in their late seventies. You're eighty-three!"

*Finish your outdoor work and get your fields ready; after that, build your house.*
PROVERBS 24:27 NIV

A man and wife were celebrating their golden wedding anniversary. After spending most of the day with relatives and friends at a party given in their honor, they returned home tired but a little hungry. They decided to have a little snack of tea and bread and butter before retiring. While the wife began making the tea, the husband opened a new loaf of bread, took out the end piece, buttered it, and handed it to his wife. He was not prepared for her reaction.

*How to be a happily married couple can never really be taught, only learned.*

"For fifty years you have been dumping the heel on me," she exploded. "I won't take this lack of concern any longer. I'm fed up with eating heels!"

Her husband stared at her in shocked dismay, then finally spoke in a small, meek voice, "But the heel on the loaf is my favorite piece."

Sometimes it takes a lifetime to learn what a spouse truly likes and dislikes. It sometimes takes that long for a person to decide what they *personally* want out of life and just exactly how they want to live. Be patient with your spouse as you "learn" all the lessons he or she embodies.

*Try to learn [in your experience] what is pleasing to the Lord [let your lives be constant proofs of what is most acceptable to Him].*
EPHESIANS 5:10 AMP

## *We need to be patient with our children in the same way God is patient with us.*

Newspaper columnist Abigail Van Buren's "Parent's Prayer" is l-o-n-g on patience!

"Oh, heavenly Father, make me a better parent. Teach me to understand my children, to listen patiently to what they have to say, and to answer all their questions kindly. Keep me from interrupting them or contradicting them. Make me as courteous to them as I would have them be to me. Forbid that I should ever laugh at their mistakes, or resort to shame or ridicule when they displease me. May I never punish them for my own selfish satisfaction or to show my power. . . . Guide me hour by hour that I may demonstrate by all I say and do that honesty produces happiness. Reduce, I pray, the meanness in me. And when I am out of sorts, help me, O Lord, to hold my tongue. May I ever be mindful that my children are children and that I should not expect of them the judgment of adults. Let me not rob them of the opportunity to wait on themselves and to make decisions. Bless me with the bigness to grant them all their reasonable requests, and the courage to deny them privileges I know will do them harm. Make me fair and just and kind. And fit me, Oh Lord, to be loved and respected and imitated by my children. Amen."

*And, fathers, do not provoke your children to anger; but bring them up in the discipline and instruction of the Lord.*
EPHESIANS 6:4 NAS

In *God Works the Night Shift,* Ron Mehl writes of Joe Knapp, who was as "fearless and aggressive as a bulldozer." He drove a beer truck down the Oregon highways and had a streak of mean in him that went clear to the bone. But Joe found the extended hand of God on a cold, snowy night in Portland, Oregon. Trying to navigate the snowy street, his beer truck stalled (of all places) in front of a church. Hearing singing from within the building, he went in and was converted that night to Christ. Joe eventually went to the mission field and became the pastor of a large Protestant church in Colombia. Joe fearlessly preached Christ. He was bombastic and tough, though his wife, Virginia, was a quiet, gracious woman.

*Nothing is so strong as gentleness. Nothing is so gentle as real strength.*

What lingered in Mehl's mind about Joe the most, however, was not his toughness, it was "his extraordinary tenderness and care shown his wife as she lay in a rest home. Joe knew she was afraid to be alone, so every day this dear man who, years earlier could have single-handedly tossed everyone out of a bar, would visit with his little wife long into the night. Every day as Joe sat at her side, he would tell her how much he loved her. . . . But most of all, he would hold her hand." Joe was strong enough to be tender.

*Thou hast also given me the shield of Thy salvation, And Thy right hand upholds me; And Thy gentleness makes me great.*
PSALM 18:35 NAS

# *If we must disagree, let's disagree without being disagreeable.*

The lyrics of a song proclaim, "I am a rock, I am an island. And a rock feels no pain, and an island never cries." Unfortunately, those who live with rocks and islands often *do* feel pain and often they do cry.

People who think of themselves as being entirely self-sufficient, are, in fact, selfish. They nearly always proclaim their opinions as the only ones that count, their feelings as the only ones that matter, their ideas as the only ones worth thinking. Such a person is rarely capable of a good argument—they simply make speeches and walk away. If you are the spouse of such a person, Dr. James Dobson offers this advice: "Change that which can be altered, explain that which can be understood, teach that which can be learned, revise that which can be improved, resolve that which can be settled, and negotiate that which is open to compromise . . . accept that which cannot be changed."

If you and your spouse cannot find an area of agreement, accept the fact that you *disagree.* Rather than suffer in silence at another's selfish tirades, simply say, "I have another point of view." Openly acknowledging your disagreement may very well be your first point of agreement!

*As far as it depends on you,*
*live at peace with everyone.*
ROMANS 12:18 AMP

Psychologists use the phrase "progressive menaces" in their professional vocabulary. This may not seem an ideal way to describe matrimony, but it does convey the idea that marriage is not static. It is ever changing. As with any normal relationship, a couple continually faces changing situations that require of each person a new orientation, a new pattern of reaction, a new way of facing life.

*Marriage is a marathon, not a sprint.*

In individual lives, our greatest years of productivity usually come later in life. Wayne Dennis at Brooklyn College studied the lives of 156 well-known scientists who lived beyond the age of seventy. He found that the decades of the forties and fifties were their most productive, with the sixties and seventies still high years of output. But their twenties were their least productive years.

Four major poets who lived beyond eighty did more work in their last decade than they did between twenty and thirty. Tennyson was eighty when he wrote "Crossing the Bar." Michelangelo painted *The Last Judgment* at age sixty-six.

The most satisfying and fulfilling years of marriage are also likely to be those that come later in life. Make your marriage one for the "long haul."

*Jacob served seven years for Rachel; and they seemed unto him* but *a few days, for the love he had to her.*

GENESIS 29:20 KJV

*Sharing the housework makes it easier to share the love.*

Joanne Kaufman says that her best friend Beth has little appreciation for the game of golf. To her, it's a boring game that takes too long to play. "Nonetheless," Joanne writes, "every weekend, three seasons out of four, she's a fixture on a certain nine-hole course near her home in upstate New York. Why? The look of sheer delight in the eyes of her husband, Jerry, when she tees off.

"'Another reason is that he would be spending those five hours without me, and I like his company,' she says. And, ultimately, lugging around a golf bag seems a small price to pay for the fact that Jerry does all the laundry—including the ironing.

"'And,' adds Beth with a smile, 'there have been other benefits.' On a recent vacation to Florida, after eighteen holes of golf in a gale force wind, her husband didn't squawk a whit about going on a major shopping expedition."

Sometimes in order to get your spouse to do what you enjoy doing, you need to do what your spouse enjoys. In the end, doing both "his and her" activities means double the amount of time spent together, rather than each person going his or her own way alone. There's something to be said for togetherness!

*Bear one another's burdens,*
*and so fulfil the law of Christ.*
GALATIANS 6:2 RSV

Bill and Lynne Hybels write in *Fit to Be Tied:* "Picture this: It is midnight. The full moon is postcard perfect and the breeze is warm. Lynne and I are sitting on a park bench at a wooded camp in Wisconsin. Twenty years old. Dating seriously. No one around . . . I wrap my arms around her. *This is what it's all about,* I think. Lynne lifts her head and looks deeply into my eyes. 'Bill, I just don't feel close to you right now'. . . . 'For heaven's sake, honey, what do you want?' I hug her a little tighter, laugh off her comment, and dismiss it from my mind.

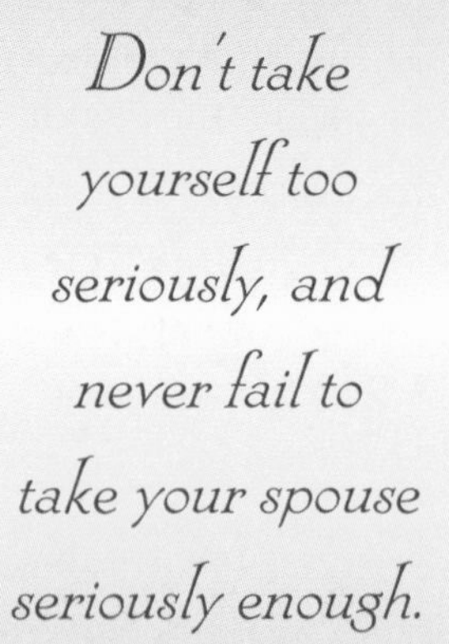


"Big mistake! If I could play that scene over, I would do it this way. I would take her hands off my shoulders, slide about a foot away, look her straight in the eye and say, 'Why don't you feel close to me? . . . If you don't know exactly why you said it, just start talking about how you feel. Maybe we can figure it out.'

"A response like that would have set a precedent for honest communication that could have made our marriage much easier. Instead we set a precedent for evasiveness, for burying feelings, for dismissing uncomfortable thoughts."

Never dismiss what your spouse says. There's a grain of truth in every joke, every sigh, every whim.

*Do nothing from selfishness or empty conceit, but with humility of mind let each of you regard one another as more important than himself.*

PHILLIPPIANS 2:3 NAS

*No marriage is all sunshine, but two people can share one umbrella if they huddle close.*

The Blue Nile is a rapidly flowing river, gaining much of its energy from the mountains from which it descends. It carries with it to the Nile delta far away, much of the rich and muddy soil from the country through which it passes.

It is joined by the White Nile, a much slower river moving across the plains. The White Nile is a clear river by comparison to the Blue.

Once joined together into the same river bed, these two rivers maintain their distinct qualities for many, many miles. From above, one can clearly see the muddy currents of the Blue Nile, and the clear waters of the White. They are separate, yet united. The longer the rivers share the same river bed, however, the more their currents intermingle until the two rivers truly become one powerful and life-giving waterway.

When tough times hit a marriage or disagreements erupt, make a decision that you will pull together, rather than allow yourself to be pulled apart by what may very well be temporary situations or resolvable differences. Choose to flow together!

*If two lie down together, then they have warmth; but how can one be warm alone?*
ECCLESIASTES 4:11 AMP

"One year after our wedding, Rosemary and I decided to spend part of the summer in Europe," writes Robert Barnes in *Rock-Solid Marriage*. "It was far from a luxury trip, as we traveled on the European rail system and stayed in hotels. One of Rosemary's dreams was to see the great art museums of Europe. One museum was enough for me. . . .

*Good listeners make good lovers.*

"It was surprising to me how much time she could spend standing in front of those paintings. They didn't mean anything to me. The difference was that she had spent part of her life being taught about the great artists of the world. . . .

"Toward the end of our stay in Europe I, too, was able to enjoy these museums because

I let her teach me about what we were looking at. Until then, we were looking at the same works of art but seeing different things.

"There's no doubt about it. Individuals enter into marriage speaking different languages. They experience things differently. They talk and listen differently. And they love and grow their self-esteem differently. Marriage can be tough unless the couple is willing to set aside some time to learn from each other."

*Listen to advice and accept instruction,*
*and in the end you will be wise.*
PROVERBS 19:20 NIV

# *It takes two to make a quarrel.*

Walter Trobisch once said, "When a couple come to me and want to get married, I always ask them if they have once had a real quarrel—not just a casual difference of opinion, but a real fight.

"Many times they will say: 'Oh no! Pastor, we love each other.'

"Then I tell them, 'Quarrel first—and then I will marry you.'

"The point is, of course, not the quarrelling, but the ability to be reconciled to each other. This ability must be trained and tested before marriage. Not sex, but rather this quarrel test, is, as I see it, a 'required' premarital experience.

"The question is, therefore: Are we able to forgive each other and to give in to each other?"

Harsh words and arguments often involve an eruption of long-harbored bitterness that is triggered by hurt feelings. We may not be able to control all the factors that lead to hurt feelings, but we each can keep bitterness from growing in our hearts. Let each day stand on its own. If an issue warrants discussion, discuss it the very day the issue arises. If you don't act upon a hurt by the day's end, consider the issue past. Burn the bridges of that hurt and don't look back on it.

*A soft answer turns away wrath,*
*But a harsh word stirs up anger.*
PROVERBS 15:1 NKJV

A man who had been married more than thirty years to his childhood sweetheart, said, "I still like to hold my wife's hand." He went on, however, to admit that he enjoyed holding his wife's hand for a different reason than he had when he was a teenager. "When we were kids," he reflected, "I got an electric spark when I touched her hand. Now my life seems filled with too much electricity, and I get a sense of peace when I hold her hand."

*A successful marriage requires falling in love many times, always with the same person.*

The touch of a hand can mean more than "I love you." Sometimes it can mean, "I care," or "I need you," or simply "I'm here."

The roots of love become branched and intertwined over time. Many sources of love and intimacy come into play. Sometimes those are rooted in compassion, sometimes in a sense of doing what is right. Sometimes they grow from giving help, other times from receiving help.

Take a fresh look at your spouse today. Find something new to appreciate. You may very well find yourself falling in love all over again!

*I will betroth you to me forever,*
*I will betroth you in righteousness*
*and justice, in love and compassion.*
HOSEA 2:19 NIV

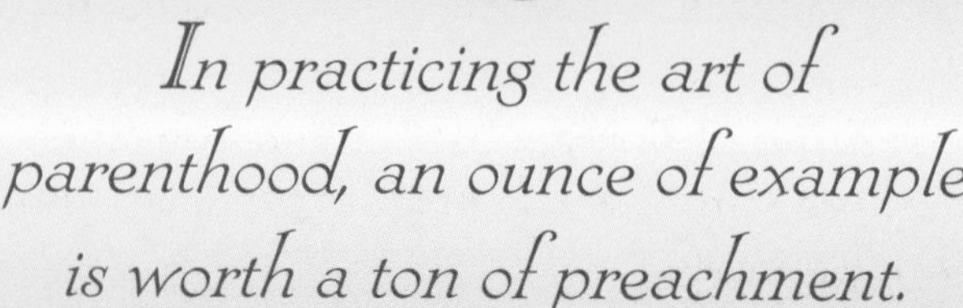

*In practicing the art of parenthood, an ounce of example is worth a ton of preachment.*

A father took his sons to an amusement park. As they stepped up to the ticket window, he asked, "How much?"

The young woman in the booth replied, "Five dollars for you and all kids twelve and over. Children eleven and younger are three dollars."

So the father said, "Well, the budding lawyer here is seven and the future doctor is twelve, so I guess I owe you thirteen dollars."

As the young woman handed him change from a $20 bill, she looked at the twelve-year-old and at his father and said, "You know you could have told me he was eleven and I would never have known the difference. You could have saved yourself a little money."

But the father replied, "That may be true, but my sons would have known the difference."

Ralph Waldo Emerson once said, "Who you are speaks so loudly I can't hear what you're saying." That is especially true as children watch and learn from their parents. Children are the best mimics in the world. They copy and repeat what they see around them, and most of what they see is behavior exhibited by Mom and Dad.

*Therefore be imitators of God,*
*as beloved children.*
Ephesians 5:1 NAS

Colleen and Louie Evans write in *My Lover, My Friend:* "Ken and Hilda were in their early sixties when we were in our twenties—and naturally we felt that sex was invented for people our age. How wrong we were! One day Hilda took me aside and said, 'Oh, Coke, since Ken has retired, we're having so much fun! We have time to do things we've wanted to do for years. We even go roller skating! And our sex life!—well, it's never been so good!' Isn't that wonderful! I gave Hilda a great big hug because I felt so happy for her—and for me, because she had expanded my limited idea of what happens to sex in the later years.

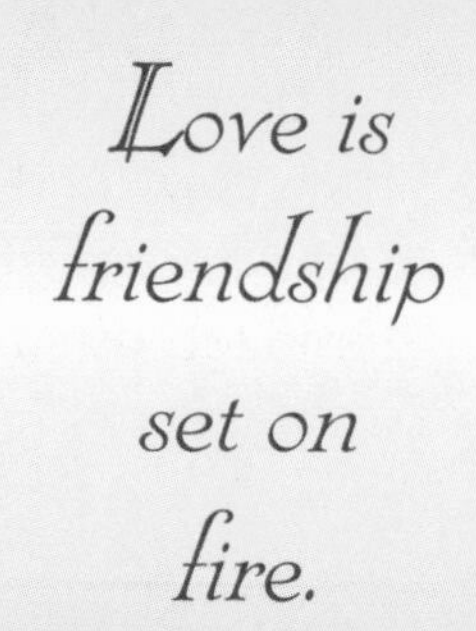


"Ken and Hilda are in their eighties now, and the miles separate us from them. But the picture and message on their Christmas card each year assure us that life is still very capable of producing a large twinkle in their eyes!"

Many young people enter marriage with what one man once described as "flaming hormones." But what those who have been married several decades often know is that physical love grows even sweeter and more satisfying as one's friendship in marriage deepens and expands. Build a friendship. It holds the key to many sparks.

*Many waters cannot quench love,*
*neither can floods drown it.*
SONG OF SOLOMON 8:7 RSV

# *Best friends make the best spouses.*

Is your spouse your best friend? How privileged you are if the answer is "yes." Perhaps an even more important question to ask is this: "Are you a good friend to your spouse?" In being a good friend, you very often gain a best friend!

A true friend is someone to whom you can empty your heart—a heart often made to feel "full" by many different sources of passion, concern, or worry.

Francis Bacon once wrote: "We know diseases of stoppings and suffocations are the most dangerous in the body; and it is not much otherwise in the mind: you may take sarza to open the liver, steel to open the spleen, flower of sulphur for the lungs, castoreum for the brain; but no receipt openeth the heart but a true friend, to whom you may impart griefs, joys, fears, hopes, suspicions, counsels, and whatsoever lieth upon the heart to oppress it, in a kind of civil shrift or confusion."

One of the best gifts you can give to your spouse and to your children is this: listening ears. Such ears are invariably connected to a kind and patient heart.

Be a friend of the four C's: compassion, caring, consideration, and comfort. Those four traits never grow old or fall out of fashion.

*There is a friend* that *sticketh closer than a brother.*
PROVERBS 18:24 KJV

"My husband had come home on the late bus from Lausanne one evening when a couple had come to have me talk to them about marriage," writes Edith Schaeffer in *What Is a Family?* "What to do? My solution was to explain, as I stopped to prepare a tray, that I felt there were priorities to be observed in married life, and that right then a very attractive meal was important. 'See how quickly I can prepare a salad with a round of pineapple on lettuce, a split banana, this orange cut in slices, a piece of cheese, some nuts on top—and this omelet! Now I'll top it off with a small pot of tea, this piece of cake, and a candle in this brass candlestick. . . . Fran will be happier by far to have me talking to you, once he has had

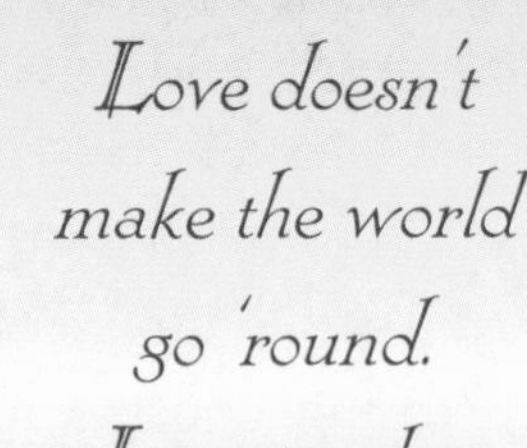

*Love doesn't make the world go 'round. Love is what makes the ride worthwhile.*

his supper, and I have spent a bit of time talking to him. I'll see you in a half an hour.'

"Then I took up the tray and spent time with Fran as he ate in our bedroom. . . . To have thrown together something not very attractive and given it to him in the room next to where we were talking would have been an irritation. Anyway, the reality of that object lesson probably would remain in the couple's memory longer than much of what I would later be saying."

*There are three things that remain—*
*faith, hope, and love–and the*
*greatest of these is love.*
I CORINTHIANS 13:13 TLB

# Lay aside life–harming heaviness and entertain a cheerful disposition.

In *The Mystery of Marriage,* Mike Mason writes about a day in which he and his wife watched a pair of hawks: "As they drew closer to us they began to descend in great lazy swoops down the blue invisible banisters of the air. . . . I parked the car, and we got out to watch. They were quite plain now. The sunlight spilled soft auras around their splayed forms. We could see frayed feathers, translucent at the tips. Not once did either bird move a wing muscle. They held themselves perfectly steady, taut yet relaxed, angling against the air and gliding as if they were part of it . . . turning in slow and beautiful spirals that meshed together and then away . . . like a pair of ice skaters.

"The longer we watched, the clearer it became that these hawks were doing absolutely nothing of any practical import: they were not hunting . . . or looking for anything, or going anywhere. They were simply playing. They were enjoying the warm blueness of the day, the strength and skill in their wings, the fun of flying . . . there was something in this soaring dance of the pair of them, with a whole sky all to themselves, which spoke directly to me, not just of play and freedom on a summer's day, but of shining beauty of love, the pure ease and joy of companionship."

*A glad heart makes a cheerful countenance,*
*but by sorrow of heart the spirit is broken.*
PROVERBS 15:13 AMP

The traditional marriage vows recited by most couples include the phrases, "in sickness and in health," "richer or poorer," and "for better or worse." There's a reason! Even the best relationships include times that qualify as sickness, poorer, and worse.

*Love is a product of habit.*

A young woman once phoned her mother and cried, "Mother, I had no idea marriage meant washing and ironing so many shirts!"

Her mother wisely counseled, "Think of each shirt you iron as an act of love." The young woman took her mother's advice and just below the neckline on each collar she ironed, she planted a big kiss, one complete with a tint of lipstick.

A marriage may involve washing and drying millions of dishes and making millions of beds, and paying thousands of bills and scrubbing the floor thousands of times. It will mean emptying the trash and mowing the lawn thousands of times, and raking perhaps billions of leaves. But if you make each mundane, "dull" chore related to your marriage an act of love, you'll find your feelings for your spouse growing ever sweeter, not more bitter.

Love in marriage means doing many things you wouldn't do otherwise. But it also involves reaping rewards you can reap in no other relationship!

*Little children, let us not love in word or speech but in deed and in truth.*

I JOHN 3:18 RSV

*After winning an argument with his wife, the wisest thing a man can do is apologize.*

Jerry Adler writes of a couple named Steve and Doreen: "Once, she said, she had an angry exchange with a clerk in a bookstore who refused to give her a refund on a book she bought a few days earlier . . . well, actually, four days earlier, which was one day more than the store allowed. But the day before was Sunday. So she was the first person in the store Monday morning, which, she thought, ought to count for something. The point, though, was that the clerk was being a total creep about it, 'and Steve just stood there smiling his patient little smile. Finally, Steve offered that instead of getting my money back we could exchange it for a book he wanted. I suppose I should have been grateful, but right at that moment I would have been happier if—$21.95 aside—he'd taken the book and shoved it sideways into the guy's mouth. . . . And I couldn't admit this to Steve, because it goes against everything I believe. . . . I was really cold to him the rest of the day. That night he said to me, 'You know, the guy was right even though he was a creep.' And after he said *that,* I didn't speak to him for three more days.'"

Giving in and agreeing, even if it flies in the face of rationality, is sometimes the better path to take.

*In the same way you married men should live considerately with [your wives], with an intelligent recognition [of the marriage relation], honoring the woman.*

I PETER 3:7 AMP

"There is something amphibious about marriage, something neither fish nor fowl," writes Mike Mason in *The Mystery of Marriage.* "It is like a three–legged sack race or a cloth–clovered dancing horse, except that it is not only the feet and body but one's whole being that gets tangled up in the other person's. Marriage is not just a sharing but a mingling of identities, a consanguinity of psyches. It is blend so intimate that it actually becomes hard to tell where one person leaves off and the other begins. People will peer and peer, for example, at a couple's offspring, trying to determine which one of the parents they resemble. Perhaps in a mysterious way what they are really trying to do is to tell the

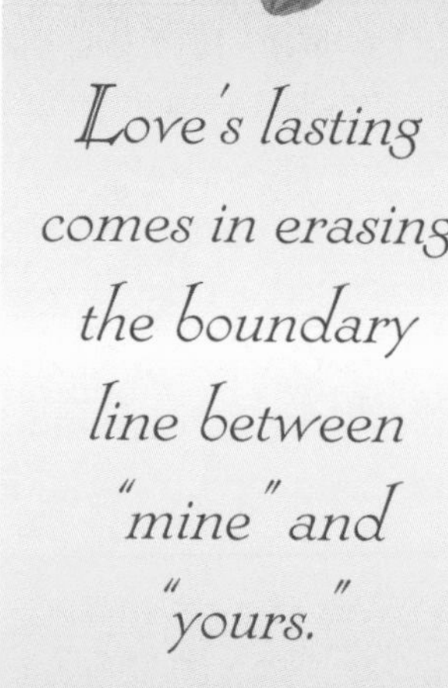

couple themselves apart, to separate again what has become impossibly intertwined. Not that this uncanny congruousness of the flesh of inner lives is always a very obvious or noticeable fact; but it becomes conspicuous in the birth of a child or at other times of crisis or exposure, at times when the hidden realities of lives float suddenly and dramatically to the surface."

*But that as a matter of equality your abundance at the present time should supply their want, so that their abundance may supply your want, that there may be equality.*

2 CORINTHIANS 8:14 RSV

# *Children don't divide a couple's love—they multiply it.*

The Bible book of Exodus tells the story of Moses' birth. As part of that story, we read how two midwives names Shiphrah and Puah were ordered by Pharaoh to kill all the male babies born to the Hebrew women. The Bible says, "But the midwives feared God, and did not do as the king of Egypt commanded them, but saved the male children alive" (Exodus 1:17 NKJV). As a result, "God dealt well with the midwives," and He provided households for them, a term that includes children. Children were their reward!

Interestingly, a famous obstetric hospital in Tel Aviv, Israel, is located today at the intersection of two streets named . . . Shiphrah Avenue and Puah Avenue.

Throughout the Bible we find that children are considered a blessing from God. In fact, to be without children—to be barren—was considered a curse. Many famous Bible stories tell how men and women prayed for children and God answered their prayers, sometimes reversing a childless situation that had lasted for decades.

The Bible does not tell a couple when to have children or how many children they should have. It doesn't command that a couple have children. The Bible says simply, "Children are a *gift* from God."

*Children are a gift from God;*
*they are his reward.*
PSALM 127:3 TLB

The marriage of Sarah and Fred was plagued by constant arguing over Fred's thoughtlessness. From his perspective, he was simply very busy in his computer-programming business, a task that took all his concentration. For her part, Sarah was fed up with his forgetting her birthday and their anniversary. "Finally," she said, "I decided that fighting with him just made things worse. So . . . I sat down and asked myself, *What other course could I take?*" She remembered how pleased Fred had been when she hugged and kissed him each time he brought her the slightest trinket. So she waited for a chance to praise him again in that way.

*Love must be learned, and learned again and again; there is no end to it.*

A few days later, Fred brought home a book she'd asked him to bring from the library. Sarah thanked him as if he had given her a diamond. "He looked at me as if I'd gone nuts," she said, "but I could tell that he knew I was pleased. After a while, I noticed that Fred actually started looking for ways to give and pay attention to me because he enjoyed being appreciated, just as it was in the early days of our courtship. For my part, I didn't care what his motivation was, I enjoyed his company and the creative things he was doing for me."

*And this I pray, that your love may abound yet more and more in knowledge and* in *all judgment.*

PHILIPPIANS 1:9 KJV

# Everyone has patience. Successful people learn to use it.

In *Traveling Hopefully,* Stan Mooneyham writes, "Early on I learned that it is a lot more fun to harvest than to hoe. Or, for that matter to plant. Few rewards can compare with that of plucking the bounty of the earth which represents the fruit of your labor. Harvesting is dramatic, fulfilling. You see what you get and you get what you see.

"Not that harvesting isn't hard work, too; but it's different. That's the payoff. The sense of reward represented by autumn's harvest can cause you to forget the less satisfying work of spring and summer. . . .

"Of course, it goes without saying that there would be no autumn harvest if there was no drudgery of spring and summer. Full barns require soil preparation, planting and hoeing. The 'winning run' in baseball may top off all the prior runs, but the first was as necessary as the final one, even if the crowds didn't leap to their feet and tear the stadium apart early in the game."

If you find yourself feeling that marriage has turned into drudgery and work, consider the possibility that life has a wonderful reward ahead. You may not see it today . . . but that reward is *growing!*

*But let patience have* her *perfect work,*
*that ye may be perfect and*
*entire, wanting nothing.*
JAMES 1:4 KJV

There's no such thing as being able to put a marriage on "automatic pilot." You may be able to preset all the dials on your microwave oven, or preset your coffee pot to have coffee upon your arising . . . but you can't preset a relationship.

*Matrimony—the high sea for which no compass has yet been invented.*

Neither is a marriage some type of rapid transit system with predictable stops along the way.

Each marriage moves in its own direction, and develops at its own pace, having its own set of obstacles.

A marriage involves a commitment, not a contract. A contract can be instantly completed, signed, sealed, and delivered. A commitment, on the other hand, is a lifetime adventure. It may begin within a few minutes, but you can never arrive at a full-blown, fully satisfying marriage quickly.

Keep in mind as you sail the high seas of your marriage that

- storms *do* abate.
- if more than one hand is on the rudder or the tiller, they need to be moving in the same direction.
- sometimes the safest thing to do is to lower the sails and let the wind take you where it will.

*There are three things too wonderful for me to understand–no four! How a ship finds its way across the heaving ocean. The growth of love between a man and a girl.*

PROVERBS 30:18 TLB

# *Marriage is not for wimps.*

Edith Schaeffer tells of a time when her husband, Francis, visited a couple only to find the husband packing to leave in the morning. He intended to run away with a girl from his workplace with whom he was infatuated. Francis spent the entire night talking to the man, even though he wasn't particularly welcome. He pointed out the many causes for their troubles and said, "Let Edith talk to your wife, then you go and *give up your job,* and go away for a three-week honeymoon." The next day, Edith spent several hours talking to his wife while she did her chores. She discovered the young woman had a stiff Mid-Victorian upbringing. So Edith advised her "to get an exotic black nightgown, some sexy underwear, some very different types of daytime clothes, have her hair done in a completely new style, buy a new kind of perfume, and go off on his planned second honeymoon determined to really forgive her husband." The two took their trip, putting each other before their material lives and staid upbringing, and they made a most amazing discovery of each other over the next three weeks.

They are grandparents today, with a beautiful family!

*Let marriage be held in honor [esteemed worthy, precious, of great price, and especially dear] inall things. And thus let the marriage bed be undefiled; for God will judge [all guilty of sexual vice].*

HEBREWS 13:4 AMP

Home has been called "heaven's fallen sister." Our home can't help but bear at least a partial imprint of our fallen world. And yet, home holds the greatest potential for being like heaven of any place on earth. A godly home, built upon heaven's principles, can be the sweetest, best, happiest, and most perfect place to be!

*A joyful marriage is a bit of heaven on earth.*

When we think of our earthly homes as being a reflection of the heavenly home of our Father, we must ask ourselves, "What must God's home be like?"

Surely it is a place where there are no harsh or unkind words, no prolonged silence born of anger. It must be a place where each person is made to feel special, important, and valued beyond measure. It is place of laughter and gladness, a place each person would desire to return to at the end of a difficult day. It must be a place of nourishment and growth, a place of total acceptance and unconditional love. Every person in God's home would surely be willing to be vulnerable and to share his or her innermost secrets, dreams, and hopes. Communication flows freely, as do hugs and kisses.

The good news is that we have the privilege of creating our homes to mirror heaven. It is within our power—with God's help—to do so!

*Enjoy life with the woman whom you love all the days of your fleeting life which He has given to you under the sun; for this is your reward in life.*

ECCLESIASTES 9:9 NAS

## *Love gives itself, it is not bought.*

*Love is the filling from one's own,*
*Another's cup,*
*Love is the daily laying down*
*And taking up;*
*A choosing of the stony path*
*Through each new day,*
*That other feet may tread with ease*
*A smoother way.*
*Love is not blind, but looks abroad*
*Through the other's eyes;*
*And asks not, "Must I give?"*
*But "May I sacrifice?"*
*Love hides its grief, that other hearts*
*And lips may sing;*
*And burdened walks, that other lives*
*May buoyant wing.*

*Hast thou a love like this?*
*Within thy soul?*
*'Twill crown thy life with bliss*
*When thou dost reach the goal.*

—Author Unknown

So many say, "I know what I need my spouse to do for me." How much wiser to have an understanding of what it is that you desire to do for your spouse!

*Many waters cannot quench love,*
*Nor will rivers overflow it; If a man were*
*to give all the riches of his house for love,*
*It would be utterly despised.*
SONG OF SOLOMON 8:7 NAS

Anne Morrow was a delicate person—not dull or incompetent, just a quiet, timid woman. Her father was ambassador to Mexico when she met a young pilot who was visiting south of the border for the U.S. State Department. He had just won a $40,000 prize for being the first pilot to fly across the Atlantic. The strong pilot and the shy princess fell deeply in love.

*A happy marriage is a long conversation which always seems too short.*

Anne could easily have been eclipsed by her husband's shadow. But rather, she wrote: "To be deeply in love is, of course, a great liberating force and the most common experience that frees. . . . Ideally, both members of a couple in love free each other to new and different worlds. I was no exception to the general rule. The sheer fact of finding myself loved was unbelievable and changed my world, my feelings about life and myself. I was given confidence, strength, and almost a new character. The man I was to marry believed in me and what I could do, and consequently I found I could do more than I realized."

Anne Morrow Lindberg became one of America's most popular authors. She and Charles had a tough, mature love tested by triumph and tragedy alike. They were married forty-seven years before death separated them—a period Anne considered far too short a time!

*Let the words of my mouth, and the meditation of my heart, be acceptable in thy sight, O Lord.*
PSALM 19:14 KJV

## *Two can live as cheaply as one—if one doesn't eat.*

Charlie Shedd writes in *Letters to Karen:* "In our married days at seminary we went often to the warehouses on grocer's row. There was one place where they stacked cans of food clear up to the ceiling. There was, however, this one difference between the cans here and those you see on your grocer's shelves. *These had no labels. . . .* The sorters had tossed them aside as "damaged," which meant anything from a major dent to some minor flaw which could only be noted by the inspector's eye. The man who ran the warehouse guaranteed this one thing—there was food of some variety in each can. He also claimed that nothing was spoiled, but, as he said, 'For three cents what you gonna lose? You pay your money and take your choice.'

"Do you know how to tell the difference between peaches and plums by the shake of a can? . . . Well, your mother and I became well-nigh infallible as shakers of edibles. Of course, no one is perfect; so we sometimes drew chili for dessert. It sounds like a fruit cocktail! Thank goodness, we had an icebox and plastic covers were cheap; so, we lived it up and laughed and ate away. In fact . . . we looked forward to our semi-monthly outing to the can hills."

*There is a right time for everything:*
*a time to laugh.*
ECCLESIASTES 3:1,4 TLB

In *The Total Woman,* Marabel Morgan gives this advice for cooling arguments before day's end:

1. *Control your tears.* When I'm mad at Charlie, I warn him ahead of time by telling him, "I'm going to get emotional. Wait a minute." Sometimes I run upstairs, cry, and feel sorry for myself. After I calm down and regain my composure, I return to carry on the conversation. I try not to sulk, nag, or refuse sex as punishment. I find that it's best to say what I have to say, and then forgive and forget.

> *Straighten your problems out before you go to bed. That way you will wake up smiling.*

2. *Plan the proper time and atmosphere.* Before you speak, think the problem through and put it into its proper perspective.
3. *Gently tell him what is in your heart.* The Bible advises us to speak the truth in love. . . . Express your emotions in words so that he'll know what's going on inside you. Your main purpose should be to make your feelings understood, not to demand change.

You can defer your anger by replacing it with understanding.

*Be angry, and* yet *do not sin; do not let the sun go down on your anger.*
Ephesians 4:26 NAS

## *Love is what you've been through with somebody.*

Within seconds after their car was hit head-on by an out-of-control vehicle, Linda knew from the silence in the back seat of the car that their daughter was either badly injured or dead. In the emergency room, Linda was told that *two* of her suspicions were confirmed: she was pregnant, and her little girl Madeline was critically injured. The next day, doctors advised Mark and Linda to disconnect Madeline's life support. She was brain dead.

Linda had heard the grim statistics about the rate of divorce among couples who had lost a child. So she and Mark promised each other from their hospital beds that they would stick together. Once home, however, they both greatly mourned the loss of their daughter and eventually had to admit they had put Madeline ahead of their relationship. A counselor helped them rebuild the foundation of their marriage. "Every day we work hard at our marriage, paying close attention to the rewards," Linda says. "The truth is that when bad things happen, you learn that the only control you have in life is how you will conduct yourself. . . . I appreciate my family for the people they are. . . . And that brings joy I never imaged I'd feel again."

*[Love] always protects, always trusts, always hopes, always perseveres.*
I CORINTHIANS 13:7 NIV

Imagine that you are in a mountain cabin high above the treeline in winter. The cabin is heated by two heaters—one on each side of the room. Over the course of the evening, after fixing dinner and settling down to read over a cup of steaming hot chocolate, you notice that you have shifted from chair to chair until you are sitting much closer to one of the heaters. The heat from your preferred heater is providing virtually all the heat you need—so much so that you can barely feel any radiance from the other heater. Upon comparing the two heaters, you find the one you are now sitting closer to has been wired into the main power source of the cabin and that the other was powered only by a small portable

> *Marriage is a promise that is shared by only two—a vow to love and dream and plan together all life through.*

generator, explaining why it is barely giving out heat after several hours of use.

Infatuation and love both seem to burn hotly at the beginning of a relationship. But ultimately, infatuation proves to be weak, as if powered by a portable generator. As time passes, its power and heat fade. Love, however, provides ongoing heat. It maintains its power and eventually, far overshadows anything infatuation may have offered.

*If two of you on earth agree (harmonize together, make a symphony together) about whatever [anything and everything] they may ask, it will come to pass* and *be done for them.*"

MATTHEW 18:19 AMP

*There's a time when you have to explain to your children why they're born, and it's a marvelous thing if you know the reason.*

In telling her story of being paralyzed as the result of a swimming accident, Joni Eareckson wrote in *Joni,* "I withdrew into myself and the solitude of home. After being away so long, I appreciated the old house with all its pleasant memories. Yet for some reason, I couldn't really feel at home there anymore; I felt awkward in my own home. . . .

"What's the matter, honey?' dad finally asked. . . .

"I sighed deeply, then said, 'I guess the thing that affects me most is that I'm so helpless. I look around the house here, and everywhere I look I see the things you've built and created. It's really sad to think that I can't leave a legacy like you'. . . .

"Dad wrinkled his forehead for a moment, then grinned again. 'You've got it all wrong. These things I've done with my hands don't mean anything. It's more important that you build character. Leave something of yourself behind. Y'see? You don't build character with your hands. . . . Maybe we'll never know the *why* of our troubles, Joni. Look—I'm not a minister or a writer—I don't know exactly how to describe what's happening to us. But, Joni, I have to believe God knows what He's doing."

For every life, there is God's purpose.

*Before I [God} formed thee in the belly I knew thee; and before thou camest forth out of the womb I sanctified thee,* and *I ordained thee.*

JEREMIAH 1:5 KJV

A man found a wallet in the street one day. There was no identification inside—only three dollars and a crumpled letter with barely legible return address on the envelope. When he opened the letter, he discovered it had been written some 60 years ago by a woman named Hannah. She was explaining to a man named Michael that her mother wouldn't allow her to see him again, but that she would always love him.

*Two souls with but a single thought, two hearts that beat as one.*

The man set out to find Hannah. He soon located her in a nursing home. She was 76 and had never married—there had just never been anyone like Michael. As the man was leaving, the doorman noticed the wallet and said, "That's Mr. Goldstein's. He's one of the old-timers on the eighth floor." The man immediately went to see Mr. Goldstein, now 78, who told him he had never married—no one had been like Hannah. The man said, "I think I know where she is" and escorted Michael down to the third floor, where he was reunited with his beloved!

Three weeks later, Michael and Hannah married, a perfect ending to a genuine love.

*A man shall leave his father and*
*mother and be joined to his wife,*
*and the two shall become one flesh.*
EPHESIANS 5:31 NKJV

# *Spouses who put their partners first have marriages that last.*

Mike Mason, author of *The Mystery of Marriage,* writes that when most people talk about the "work" of marriage, they primarily mean "precious time." He says, "It is like the amount of fuel that must be fed into a big powerful, shiny, eight-cylinder gas guzzler that has to be kept constantly on the road. You cannot leave a marriage sitting in the driveway even for a day, because the only reason for marriage is togetherness. It is an alliance of love, and love is a spiritual vehicle, rocket ship, that travels faster and farther than anything else under the sun.

"Get out of it for a moment, and it leaves without you for parts unknown; let it idle, and it begins to rust; neglect it, and it seizes right up. It can be a full-time job just being a passenger in this thing. But like it or not, you and your spouse are in it together, and in it for life, and the work of traveling in marriage is the most vital work you can do. In the Lord's plans for the world there is no work more important than the work of relationship, and no relationship is more important than that of one's marriage."

*But in lowliness of mind let each esteem other better than themselves.*
PHILIPPIANS 2:3 KJV

A popular ad slogan in recent years has been "Together we can do it." That's a good motto to have in marriage. Marriage is a partnership. It is not a matter of one ruling over another, or of two people going their separate ways and occasionally touching base. A partnership means that each person is equally responsible for the whole.

*Successful marriages usually rest on a foundation of accountability between husbands and wives.*

In business, partners rarely are involved in identical activities. One may be in charge of marketing, while the other is in charge of manufacturing. One may manage the finances, while the other manages personnel. Each function, however distinct or visible, is vital to the success of the business. The same is true in a marriage. Each spouse usually has different responsibilities—

all of which are vitally important to the success of the relationship.

A business partnership will fail miserably if the partners fail to communicate. They must have goals to which they both agree. They must be able to "create" their business together with a sense of mutual commitment. Again, the same is true for marriage! Communication is a must, and shared goals are what will give hope and life to your relationship.

*Together, you CAN have a marriage partnership.*

*Submitting yourselves one to another in the fear of God.*
EPHESIANS 5:21 KJV

*What greater thing is there for two human souls than to feel that they are joined for life.*

Ray Rosa grew up in Italy and came to the United States as a young man in 1921. He met and married his wife, Isabel, and they settled in Swampscott, Massachusetts, where Ray worked as a barber most of his life. Three years ago, Isabel became ill and was moved to a nursing home in a nearby town.

Ray's routine dramatically changed. Seven mornings a week, he would take the 10:25 bus to the nursing home, where he would stay until 5:30 in the afternoon. Isabel is waiting for him in a wheelchair each morning. They spend the day together, Ray helps Isabel with her needs, occasionally brings his mandoline and sings Italian songs for the other patients at the home. He usually gives a haircut or two to some of the men patients and regales them with stories of his career. To those in the nursing home, Ray is a hero, a bright aspect on any day, a source of warmth and laughter and encouragement.

From Ray's perspective, he's simply fulfilling a promise he made years ago, one that said "in sickness and in health."

*"What therefore God hath joined together, let not man put asunder."*
MATTHEW 19:6 KJV

Have you ever watched puppies and kittens at play? They growl and snarl at each other, occasionally jump at each other. They seem a constant blur of fur in motion—cuffing at one another, rolling, tumbling, grabbing, chewing, scampering. Puppies and kittens seem to have an endless capacity for rough-and-tumble play.

*Be careful that your marriage doesn't become a duel instead of a duet.*

But occasionally, one in the group will go too far. And that's when "the fur flies." What was once friendly banter turns into serious confrontation and a battle for turf. The growls become a little harsher, the blows are a little harder. The atmosphere changes to one of intensity. Often, the mother dog or cat must step in to break up the scuffle and give the young offenders a sound rebuke.

Most quarrels in marriage begin with just a word or two that goes "over the line" from banter to badger, from nudge to nag, from comment to criticism. Quarrels nearly always lead to a perceived need for retaliation, justification, recrimination. They destroy not only the peace between two people, but the inner peace of both parties involved.

Choose your words carefully.

*Let us therefore follow after the things which make for peace, and things wherewith one may edify another.*
ROMANS 14:19 KJV

*You can send your marriage to an early grave with a series of little digs.*

A golden anniversary party was once given in honor of an elderly couple. The husband was moved by the many gestures of love that they had received from their family and friends. He stood to give a toast to his wife, saying, "My dear wife, after fifty years I've found you tried and true!" Everyone smiled approval, but his wife, who was hard of hearing, responded, "Eh?"

He repeated louder, "AFTER FIFTY YEARS I'VE FOUND YOU TRIED AND TRUE!"

His wife bristled and immediately shot back, "Well, let me tell you something—after fifty years I'm tired of you too!"

Little barbs are just that—barbs. They are like the twisted bits of wire found on a barbed-wire fence. While a fence may be a good thing in terms of setting boundaries to a relationship, giving a sense of security and protection, barbs are a reminder that the relationship is one that has pain associated with it. Even teasing that begins in fun can end up being an irritant. So, too, are cutting cynical and sarcastic remarks, prickly unkind comments, and pointed jokes.

Very often the key to improved communication is the removal of barbs and the filling in of "digs."

*Death and life* are *in the power of the tongue: and they that love it shall eat the fruit thereof.*
PROVERBS 18:21 KJV

In his best-seller *Maybe (Maybe Not),* Robert Fulghum tells the story of a couple who had agreed prior to marriage that they would either have children or pets, but not both. Two daughters later, Tom thought their deal was secure until his wife helped organize an auction to raise money for their daughter's school. She planned to use her own expertise in raising dogs as a way of providing a valuable item for the event. So she went to the pound and brought home a puppy, intending to contribute it to the cause.

*Love is the condition in which the happiness of another person is essential to your own.*

As soon as the dog had gone on the block, Fulghum writes, "There is a sniffle from the mother. Tears are running down her face and the dog is licking the tears off her cheeks. In a whisper not really meant for public notice, the mother calls to her husband: 'Tom, Tom, I can't sell this dog—I want this dog—he loves me—I love him—oh, Tom.' Every eye in the room is on this soapy drama. The father feels ill, realizing the great bowling ball of fate is headed down his alley. At that moment, everybody in the room knows who is going to buy the pooch. The dog is going home with Tom." Fulghum concludes: "I say he got off light. It could have been ponies or llamas or pot-bellied pigs."

*[Love] does not seek its own.*

I CORINTHIANS 13:5 NAS

*Being married teaches us at least one very valuable lesson— to think before we speak.*

Thank You, God, for teaching us to talk to one another. Thank You for the gift of words.

Thank You for giving us each other with whom to share our hopes, our fears, our problems and our plans.

Thank You for the assurance, that since there is no fear in love, we can be totally honest, completely ourselves, without the risk of ridicule or rejection.

Thank You for showing us the need to listen. To listen with our hearts as well as with our ears. To sense the needs that may remain unspoken beneath a torrent of words. And to know that when there are no words to meet the situation, love can be a silent song—a touch that says, 'I'm in this situation with you,' a smile that reassures, 'You're doing fine.'

Thank You that we have learned the need for patience. The discipline to talk things through until both minds are satisfied. Even if we then return to the original solution!

Thank You for teaching a talkative partner brevity, and a quiet one how to express himself.

Thank You, God, for teaching us to talk to one another. Thank You for the gift of words.

—Marion Stroud, *The Gift of Marriage*

*A word aptly spoken is like*
*apples of gold in settings of silver.*
PROVERBS 25:11 NIV

In Bible times, apartment-style homes were built atop city walls. Part of the roof extended beyond the walls to protect them from rain and sun. The word for this overhang is translated, "forbear," in English. It literally means to "outroof." This is the way God commands us to love—to forbear one another in love, or to "outroof" one another—to protect those you love with your love, rather than expose them and their faults.

> *A good marriage is . . . a relationship where healthy perspective overlooks a multitude of "unresolvables."*

This does not mean we are to be blind to error or to live in a state of denial about wrongs committed around or to us. It means simply we choose to love so much that our love overshadows the hurt those wrongs may have done. We recognize that we can never know the "whole story" about another person or event. We can only know so much about their motives or inner heart. However, we can choose not to focus on those things we don't understand and can focus instead on what we can do: love.

As one old minister once told his country congregation, "God invites us to be His partner in everything but judging people."

*Above all, love each other deeply, because love covers over a multitude of sins.*
I PETER 4:8 NIV

*Let the wife make the husband glad to come home, and let him make her sorry to see him leave.*

A pastor once had a man come into his office and say, "I want what my wife has found."

The pastor asked, "What do you think it is that she found?"

The man replied, "I'm not sure, but whatever it is, it sure has changed her disposition."

This man's wife had been a difficult, demanding person. She had found it excruciating to give without receiving twice as much in return. Her needs kept the family dynamics constantly in turmoil. She could be extremely unpleasant when things didn't go as *she* had planned or if her demands weren't met.

What had happened? She started attending an Enabler's Group in her neighborhood. The women, all members of the same church, opened their hearts to this woman. One day at the end of a meeting she stayed to talk with one of the women about her life. Facing the fact of her rotten disposition she prayed, almost as an experiment: "Christ, if You are alive as these people say You are, help me to change." The result of that prayer came slowly but surely. She repeated the prayer each morning, and within just a few months, her husband had not only noticed the difference, but wanted the same!

How's your disposition doing these days?

*Let each man of you [without exception]*
*love his wife as [being in a sense] his*
*very own self; and let the wife see that*
*she respects* and *reverences her husband*
*[that she notices him, regards him].*
EPHESIANS 5:33 AMP

As the ancient myth goes, when Ulysses sailed out to meet the Sirens, he stopped his ears with wax and had himself bound to the mast of his ship. He was apparently unaware that every traveller before him had done the same thing and that wax and chains were no match for the Sirens. Their alluring song could pierce through everything causing sailors to break all manner of bonds.

*Watch out for temptation—the more you see of it the better it looks.*

The Sirens, however, had a more fatal weapon than their song. It was silence. As Ulysses approached them, the Sirens chose to employ that weapon. Rather than be seduced into straining to hear their song, Ulysses concluded that he alone must be the only person who could not hear their song and that he must be immune to their powers. Strengthened in that confidence, he set his gaze on the distant horizon and escaped the Sirens as no man before him.

Temptation always lies first in what we see and what we hear. Choose carefully where your eyes and ears wander.

*"Keep watching and praying that you may not come into temptation."*
MARK 14:38 NAS

*Forgiveness means giving up your right to punish another.*

In 1946, Czeslaw Godlewski was a member of a gang of youths that roamed and sacked the German countryside. On one isolated farm, they gunned down ten members of the Hamelmann family. Nine of them died. But the father, Wilhelm, miraculously survived his four bullet wounds.

As the time approached for Godlewski to complete his twenty-year prison term for his crimes, the state would not release him because he simply had nowhere to go. None of his family members offered shelter, and each place the state sought to place him refused to take him. Then a letter was received by the warden. In it was a simple request, "I ask you to release Godlewski to my custody and care. Christ died for my sins and forgave me. Should I not then forgive this man?" The letter was signed, Wilhelm Hamelmann.

Lord Balfour once advised, "The best thing to give to your enemy is forgiveness; to an opponent, tolerance." If these are the best we can give to our enemies and opponents, how much more should we grant forgiveness and tolerance to those we love!

*"And when you stand praying,*
*if you hold anything against anyone,*
*forgive him, so that your Father in*
*heaven may forgive you your sins."*
MARK 11:25 NIV

To say that Tina's husband was tight with money would have been an understatement. A friend once said to him, "Jack, you can squeeze a penny so hard it cries." Tina, on the other hand, enjoyed an occasional splurge or impulse purchase.

*The difficulty with marriage is that we fall in love with a personality, but must live with a character.*

After they married, Jack insisted that Tina account for every penny she spent and that she consult with him on any expenditure over $5. She went along with this dictum for a few months, but eventually felt such strict control was destroying her spontaneity and sense of fun in life. So she issued an ultimatum to Jack: "Give me a household allowance, but don't question my use of a single penny of it."

At first, Jack was frightened to lose control. What if Tina overspent and he had to come up with even more than he had agreed upon? Tina reminded him that she had once managed her own money quite nicely. So Jack agreed to give the new plan a 90-day trial.

At the end of the three-month period, Jack not only admitted that he enjoyed the surprises Tina brought into their life, but he increased the amount of money he allowed her to manage. And within two years, Jack was giving *himself* an allowance and turning the rest of their budget over to Tina.

*Confess* your *faults one to another,*
*and pray one for another.*
JAMES 5:16 KJV

*It doesn't matter who you marry, for you are sure to find out the next morning that it was someone else.*

In *Magnificent Marriage,* Gordon MacDonald writes: "Conflict of a destructive sort breeds quickly if there is an inability to accept our partner as he really is. A dangerous marital game is called "Why can't you be like?' . . . It can work with effective force from both sides. The wife who knows that her husband is always comparing her appearance with another woman is hurt just as badly as the man who knows that he is being compared with another man who can afford to take his family to Bermuda every spring vacation.

"It was Keith Miller who first made me aware of this fatal cancer of relationship. . . . 'In retrospect, I think Mary Allen's vision of a husband was a perfectly balanced blend of big John Wayne, Jack Parr, and Father Flanagan. But in all honesty, I think my premarital vision of an ideal wife was probably a combination of St. Theresa, Elizabeth Taylor, and . . . Betty Crocker'. . . . Miller formed new depths to their companionship when he learned to love his wife for exactly what she was and not some plastic model of what he wished for her to be."

Our best prayer is not "Lord, You love him and I'll change him," but "Lord, You change him and I'll love him."

*I will betroth you to me in faithfulness*
*and love, and you will really know*
*me then as you never have before.*
HOSEA 2:20 TLB

A man who had just arrived in Heaven could hardly stop telling St. Peter how grateful he was to be in such a glorious place. He asked Peter to give him one glimpse into Hades so that he might further appreciate his good fortune, and Peter allowed this.

*Love is giving more and never keeping score.*

In Hades he saw a long table extending as far as his eye could behold. The table was covered with the most delicious and varied foods the man had ever seen. Yet, everyone seated around the table was starving. The man asked Peter, "Why don't they eat?"

Peter replied, "Everyone is required to take food from the table only with four-foot-long forks. They are so long that no one can reach the food from the table to his mouth, and therefore each one is slowly dying."

Upon his return to Heaven, the man saw a table that appeared identical! It, too, was laden with delicious foods of every type. Yet the people around this table were well fed. The man said to Peter, "They must have much shorter forks here in Heaven!"

Peter replied, "No, only four-foot-long forks."

Puzzled, the man asked, "Then why are those in Hades starving to death and those in Heaven seem to be happy and well fed?"

Peter replied, "In Heaven, people feed each other."

*[Love] takes no account of the evil done to it [it pays no attention to a suffered wrong].*

I CORINTHIANS 13:5 AMP

## *The best comforter isn't a down-filled quilt.*

In *Women Who Do Too Much,* Patricia Sprinkle writes: "Three months before I spoke with Nancy, her husband lost a four-year battle to a degenerative brain disease. She said, 'This was a brilliant man, a gentle man, a man with a terrific sense of humor. I grieved as he lost his ability to walk, pick up things from the floor, write, speak clearly. We had been married for thirty years and expected to grow old together. Suddenly, in one day, our life changed. He flew to Mayo clinic one morning and called me that night with the doctor's diagnosis. They could do nothing for him.

"'I remember thinking after I hung up on the phone, *life is never going to be the same again*. Nobody gets a rehearsal for this. You don't get to practice.

"'I was furious with God—banged my fist on many tables. But I learned to thank God that God is God. God didn't get bowled over by my fury. Instead, He told me, 'I won't leave you. I'm as sad about this as you are. I grieve with you.' The shared grief of God gets me through my own.'"

Jesus called the Holy Spirit the "Comforter." He alone is with us *every* moment of our lives.

*Even though I walk through*
*the valley of the shadow of death,*
*I fear no evil; for Thou art with me;*
*Thy rod and Thy staff, they comfort me.*
PSALM 23:4 NAS

Lewis Smedes of Fuller Theological Seminary once shared with a congregation: "May I share with you some reasons why I believe? All good reasons, none of them the really real reason. There's my family. I believe because I was brought up in a believing family. I don't make any bones about that. I don't know what would have happened to me if I had been born in the depth of Manchuria of a Chinese family. I just don't know. I do know that I was led to believe in the love of God as soon as I learned I should eat my oatmeal. We did a lot of believing in our house. We didn't have much else to do, as a matter of fact. Other kids sang 'Jesus loves me this I know, 'cause the Bible tells me so.' I sang, 'Jesus

*No man or woman is a failure who has helped hold a home happily together. He who has been victorious in his home can never by completely defeated.*

loves me this I know, 'cause my ma told me so.'

"I wasn't alone. You probably heard about a reporter asking the great German theologian, Karl Barth, toward the end of his career: 'Sir, you've written these great volumes about God, great learned tomes about all the difficult problems of God. How do you know they're all true?' And the great theologian smiled and said, 'Cause my mother said so!'

"Families are God's primary missionary society."

*Blessed is the man whose quiver is full of them; They shall not be ashamed, When they speak with their enemies in the gate.*

PSALM 127:5 NAS

*The key to a healthy marriage is to keep your eyes wide open before you wed . . . and half closed thereafter.*

Columnist Ann Landers has offered some excellent advice about the difference between infatuation and love: "Infatuation is instant desire. It is one set of glands calling to another. Love is friendship that has caught fire. It takes root and grows—one day at a time.

"Infatuation is marked by a feeling of insecurity. You are excited and eager, but not genuinely happy. There are nagging doubts, unanswered questions, little bits and pieces about your beloved that you would just as soon not examine too closely. It might spoil the dream.

"Love is quiet understanding and the mature acceptance of imperfection. . . .

"Infatuation says, 'We must get married right away. I can't risk losing him.' Love says, 'Be patient. Don't panic. Plan your future with confidence.'

"Infatuation lacks confidence. When he's away, you wonder if he's cheating. . . . Love means trust. You are calm, secure and unthreatened. . . .

"Infatuation might lead you to do things you'll regret later, but love never will. Love is an upper. It makes you look up. It makes you think up. It makes you a better person than you were before."

*Be kind to one another, tenderhearted,*
*forgiving one another, even as*
*God in Christ also forgave you.*
EPHESIANS 4:32 NKJV

Pamela, from Europe, met her husband Steve while they were both traveling in Israel. After a romantic, whirlwind courtship, they married. Within three years, Pam found herself living in a small town in the United States, caring for two babies. The hardest part of the transition in her life, however, was the change she saw in Steve. He worked long hours, stayed out late with friends, and did little to help her with the children. He complained that she nagged him and balked at any suggestion he change.

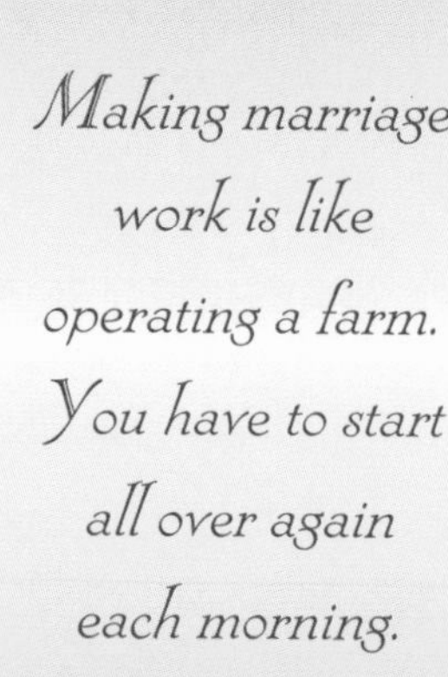


A counselor helped Pam take a look at her own life. She soon recognized that there was a difference in her own behavior in their getting-along times and their times of conflict. In a nutshell, when Pam was nice to Steve, he was nice to her. With this new awareness, Pam set about to change her ways. When Steve came home late, she didn't protest. She simply asked how his day had gone. Before too many days, Pam noticed that Steve was coming home earlier. Then one Saturday, he got up early to take care of the children so she could sleep in. She was thrilled.

Are *you* the same person you used to be? That may be a good question to ask if you feel that one of you in the relationship has "changed."

*Cause me to hear Your lovingkindness*
*in the morning, For in You do I trust.*
PSALM 143:8 NKJV

*Married couples who claim they have never had an argument in forty years either have poor memories or a very dull life to recall.*

Given the unique intimacies and experiences of marriage, it's no wonder couples face arguments and anger in their relationship. Learning to deal with anger, though, can defuse a potential battleground.

In *Marriage in the Making,* Richard Exley describes the three basic ways we tend to deal with anger: "*Express it*—let it all hang out! . . . I've witnessed the consequences of this flawed strategy on numerous occasions . . . family fights . . . abused children . . . battered wives.

"*Repress it*—deny your feelings! Pretend that you are not angry at all. People who handle their anger by repressing it subsequently suffer any number of physical and psychological symptoms . . . ranging from a spastic colon, an ulcer, a rash or even a heart attack.

"The third, and most effective, way of dealing with your anger is to own it. *Confess it*—acknowledge your feelings! Take responsibility for them . . . process them in an appropriate way. . . . Many people have found prayer to be a safe and effective way of expressing their angry thoughts and feelings. Once they tell God how they feel, and why they are angry, their anger is usually under control. An additional benefit is the insight they often receive while in prayer."

*Faithful are the wounds of a friend, but the kisses of an enemy are lavish* and *deceitful.*
PROVERBS 27:6 AMP

A painting by Murillo hangs in the Louvre in Paris. It is entitled *The Miracle of San Diego.* In it, an open door is depicted, with two noblemen and a priest entering a kitchen. They are astonished to find that all of the kitchen maids are angels. One maid is handling a water pot, another a large piece of meat, a third a basket of vegetables. The fourth angel maid is tending the fire.

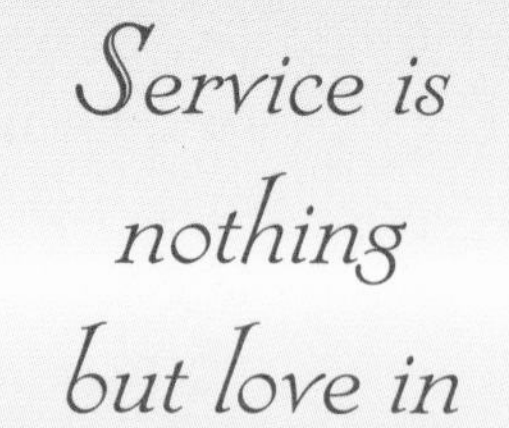


What a wonderful image that in the eyes of the Lord, no labor is beneath dignity and no laborer is "common."

Make your home a place of service to others—a place to pray as you work, share as you relax, and witness as you serve.

*As we partake of earthly food*

*When the table for us is spread,*
*We'll not forget to thank Thee, Lord,*
*Who gives us daily bread.*
*So bless my little kitchen, God,*
*And those who enter in;*
*May they find naught but joy and peace*
*And happiness therein.*

*"The more lowly your service*
*to others, the greater you are.*
*To be the greatest, be a servant."*
MATTHEW 23:11 TLB

# *You keep a lifetime commitment by keeping promises day by day.*

Contrary to what many people think, rules usually don't limit and prohibit what a person desires to do as much as they provide security and a sense of sure predictability for those who live within them. The patterns of behavior, habits, and rituals a couple develops during their marriage provide structure and assurance. They become the "norms" on which both people can count.

Two parents once made a decision to not allow their children to watch any scary movies on television. Then one night while Mom was out shopping, Dad noticed an old black-and-white horror movie in the TV listings he had enjoyed as a child. The children saw the listing too and remembered that Dad had once told them about the movie. "Please!" they pleaded. "We promise we won't tell Mom."

However, Dad remembered his own promise to Mom, "Your Mom and I agreed on this," he said. "I owe it to her to keep my end of the deal." Not only did Dad keep his children from a few potential nightmares that night, he gave them a great lesson in what it means to make a commitment—and keep it.

Keeping the rules of a relationship may very well result in . . . keeping the relationship!

*"But let your statement be, 'Yes, yes' or 'No, no'; and anything beyond these is of evil."*
MATTHEW 5:37 NAS

The Agassiz brothers lived in a home on the shore of a lake in Switzerland. One winter day, the boys' father was on the lake's other side, and the boys pleaded with their mother for the privilege of setting out across the lake to join him. Their mother knew the lake was covered with thick ice, so she bundled them up, then stood in their doorway to watch them as they made their way across the ice. She became alarmed when she realized they had come to a crack in the ice. The older boy jumped over the crack easily, but the younger one was afraid. As the mother watched, she saw the older brother get down on his face and stretch his body over the crack to make a bridge of himself. The younger brother crept

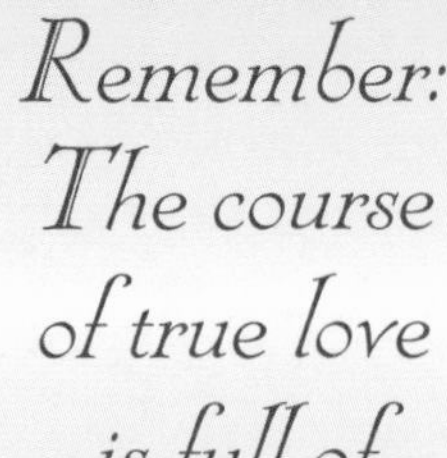

*Remember: The course of true love is full of obstacles.*

over his still form, slowly but surely, then the older brother stood, and they proceeded safely on their way.

In any marriage, one or the other spouse is going to encounter a chasm or an obstacle that hinders or causes fear. It is in these times that the other spouse must find a way to "bridge the gap"—sometimes enduring hardship and sometimes merely exhibiting patient lovingkindness—until the two can walk together again in wholeness.

*For you have need of endurance, so that*
*after you have done the will of God,*
*you may receive the promise.*
HEBREWS 10:36 NKJV

*It is such a comfort to drop the tangles of life into God's hands and leave them there.*

A local parks commission was once ordered to remove the trees from a certain street so the street could be widened. As the tree removers were about to begin their work, the foreman noticed a robin's nest in one of the trees with the mother robin sitting on it. The foreman ordered his crew to leave the tree for later removal.

When the workers returned to the tree, they found the nest still occupied with wide-mouthed baby robins. Again, they left the tree.

When they returned two weeks later, they found the nest empty. The family of baby robins had grown and flown away. Something in the bottom of the nest caught the eye of one of the workmen. It was a little white card, soiled yet still legible. As the worker separated it from the mud and sticks used to make the rest of the nest, he found that it was a small Sunday school card. On it were these words: "We trust in the Lord our God."

The greatest surety that we have for the resolution of our worries and cares is to leave them with the Lord.

*Cast your cares on the LORD*
*and he will sustain you.*
PSALM 55:22 NIV

Roger and Emily had been happily married for fourteen years when tragedy struck: Emily was diagnosed with breast cancer. She underwent extensive chemotherapy, a mastectomy, and then still more chemotherapy. Three years after her ordeal, friends gave Emily a "third-anniversary" party following an "all clear" series of tests that showed no recurrence of the disease in her life. "Roger was there for me every step of the way," Emily shared with those who had gathered with them to celebrate.

*The difference between smooth sailing and shipwreck in marriage lies in what you as a couple are doing about the rough weather.*

"Were you surprised?" a friend asked jokingly.

"Not at all," Emily said. "But the doctor told me that many husbands are unable to stay with their wives during chemotherapy treatments. Many women come with a female relative or friend. Roger always came with me."

"Was this the worst crisis in your marriage?" another friend asked.

"Absolutely," Roger replied. "I couldn't even hear to think that I might lose Emily."

Emily added, "I said earlier that Roger was there for me every step of the way. The point is—we took this as we have taken all things in our marriage: step by step. Some steps are harder than others—but each is still just that, a step."

*If thou faint in the day of adversity, thy strength is small.*

PROVERBS 24:10 KJV

*Married life is a marathon. It is not enough to make a great start toward a long-term marriage. You need determination.*

Marathon runners learn several important lessons as they train for their sport over the years. One is that a calamity can happen at virtually any time. No matter how experienced a runner may be, a small stone in the path, a misstep, a distraction, or any other of a myriad of hindrances can occur at any time, breaking the runner's stride and causing an accident or injury. So, too, in marriage. The length of a marriage does not provide immunity from problems.

Marathon runners learn to pace themselves and not to burn themselves out during the first few miles of a race. So, too, couples are wise to see their relationship as one for the "long run" and to put all problems and differences into the perspective of a bigger picture.

Finally, marathon runners—with the exception of the handful at the very top of the sport—eventually compete against their own best times. They are not truly in competition with other runners. They run to complete a race and to do *their* best. Competition can ruin a relationship. The far better approach is for each person to work on becoming the best he or she can be, and to work on making their relationship the best it can be.

*You need to keep on patiently doing*
*God's will if you want him to do*
*for you all that he has promised.*
HEBREWS 10:36 TLB

J. C. Macaulay once took a group of his college students who were preparing for Christian service on the mission field to the famous Biltmore Estate near Asheville, North Carolina. He was eager to see their response to the vast wealth of the grounds, and he was hopeful that his students would confront any materialistic desires that they might have before they went abroad.

*Real joy comes not from riches or from the praise of men but from doing something worthwhile.*

He watched as the students viewed the fabulous treasures on display, moving from one luxurious room to another. Several of the students commented on the value of various items. Others remarked about the exquisite perfection of various artifacts and pieces of furniture. All showed a great appreciation for the upkeep of the spacious and beautiful grounds.

His heart was warmed, though, when, as they returned from the trip, the students spontaneously began to sing the words of an old hymn:

*When you look at others with their lands and gold,*
*Think that Christ has promised you His wealth untold;*
*Count your blessings—money cannot buy*
*Your reward in Heaven nor your home on high.*

*"It is more blessed to give than to receive."*
ACTS 20:35 NIV

*Courtesy costs nothing,*
*yet it buys things*
*that are priceless.*

While on vacation in New England the year after they were married, Sue and Kevin purchased two red "You're Special" plates at an outlet mall. They like them so much they decided to use them as their "everyday dishes." Then one day, one of the plates broke. That night, Kevin said, "You should get the special plate tonight."

"Why?" Sue asked. "Because you finished that big project that you were working on."

The next night, Sue insisted that Kevin dine from the "You're Special" plate, in honor of the help he had given to a neighbor in need. Thereafter, Sue and Kevin vied nightly for the "You're Special" plate honors—not to *receive* the plate, but for the privilege of awarding it to the other!

When the plate finally broke, Sue said sadly, "I had never been affirmed as much in my entire life as I was those eight months that Kevin and I bestowed upon each other the 'You're Special' honors. What seemed like courtesy the first night Kevin gave me the plate actually set a precedent for our encouraging each other on a daily basis. We're looking for another set of plates now—including one for the baby that's on the way!"

*To sum up, let all be harmonious, sympathetic, brotherly, kindhearted, and humble in spirit.*

I PETER 3:8 NAS

"From the moment I met my wife," Mike Mason writes in *The Mystery of Marriage,* "I sensed that a process of interior disintegration was beginning to work in me, systematically, insidiously. In other ways, of course, I was being rejuvenated, tremendously built up. But a thirty-year-old man is like a densely populated city: nothing new can be built, in its heart, without something else being torn down. So I began to be demolished. There were many times when I felt quite seriously that everything my life had stood for was being challenged, or that somehow I had been tricked into selling my very soul for the sake of a woman's love! . . . There was a lot at stake as the wedding day approached: in fact, there was everything at

*You can never be happily married to another until you get a divorce from yourself. Successful marriage demands a certain death to self.*

stake. Never before had I felt that so much was riding upon one single decision. Later I would discover . . . that that is one of the chief characteristics of love: it asks for everything. Not just a little bit, or a whole lot, but for everything. . . .

"In marriage the breaking that is done is done by the very heel of love itself. It is not physical pain or natural disaster or the terrible evil world 'out there' that is to blame, but rather it is love, love itself that breaks us."

*And they that are Christ's have crucified the flesh with the affections and lusts. If we live in the Spirit, let us also walk in the Spirit.*

GALATIANS 5:24,25 KJV

*Love is the one business in which it pays to be an absolute spendthrift: Give it away; splash it over; empty your pockets; shake the basket; and tomorrow you'll have more than ever.*

Love is often called the "queen" of the fruit of the Spirit, the supreme manifestation of the Christian character. Donald Grey Barnhouse has made this very clear in his description of the fruit of the Spirit (see Galatians 5:22,23):

*Love is the key.*
*Joy is love singing.*
*Peace is love resting.*
*Longsuffering is love enduring.*
*Kindness is love's touch.*
*Goodness is love's character.*
*Faithfulness is love's habit.*
*Gentleness is love's self-forgetfulness.*
*Self-control is love holding the reins.*

Marriage is usually founded upon love. Sustaining that love is an ongoing daily privilege. Begin and end each day with words of love and acts of kindness for each other. Don't be like the man who responded to his wife when she complained that he never told her he loved her: "I told you I loved you on our wedding day, and if I ever change my mind, I'll let you know." Rather, share your expressions of love generously and frequently!

*"Give, and it will be given to you.*
*A good measure, pressed down,*
*shaken together and running over,*
*will be poured into your lap. For with the*
*measure you use, it will be measured to you."*
LUKE 6:38 NIV

The children of a very wealthy family were put into the care of a very qualified nanny, as well as a host of other servants the family employed. When adverse market trends impacted the family's finances, the family moved into a slightly smaller home, but they kept the children's nanny. Eventually, however, the family's financial situation became severe enough that they had to let the beloved nanny go.

*Superfluous wealth can buy superfluities only. Money is not required to buy one necessity of the soul.*

Then one evening after the father returned home from a day of great anxiety and business worry, his little girl climbed up on his knee and threw her arms around his neck. "I love you, papa," she said, trying to soothe the weariness she intuitively perceived in him.

"I love you, too, darling," the father replied, glad to have such a warm welcome home.

The little girl then said, "Papa, will you make me a promise?"

The father said, "What is it?"

So she said, "Papa, please promise me you won't get rich again. You never came to see us when you were rich, but now we can see you every night and hug you and kiss you and climb on your knee. Please don't get rich again!"

*Wealth is worthless in the day of wrath,*
*but righteousness delivers from death.*
PROVERBS 11:4 NIV

*Friendship improves happiness, and abates misery, by doubling our joy, and dividing our grief.*

A friend is someone you are comfortable with, someone whose company you prefer. A friend is someone you can count on. . . .

A friend is one who believes in you . . . someone with whom you can share your dreams. In fact, a real friend is a person you want to share all of life with—and the sharing doubles the fun.

When you are hurting and you can share your struggles with a friend, it eases the pain. A friend offers you safety and trust. . . .

A friend will pray with you . . . and for you.

My friend is someone with whom I can share my ideas and philosophies, someone with whom I can grow intellectually. . . .

My friend is one who hears my cry of pain, who senses my struggle, who shares my lows as well as my highs.

My friend does not always say I am right, because sometimes I am not. . . .

My lover, my friend—this is what a marriage partner should be.

—Colleen Evans

*A friend loves at all times, and*
*a brother is born for adversity.*
PROVERBS 17:17 NIV

Francis of Assisi had a secret fear—he was terrified of leprosy. One day as he was traveling alone on foot to another place of ministry, he encountered on the narrow path ahead of him a figure horribly white in the sunshine—a leper! Instinctively, his heart shrank back and he considered for an instant how he might graciously turn around and hurry in the opposite direction. He feared his face had already shown how inside he was recoiling at the thought of being contaminated by the dreadful disease.

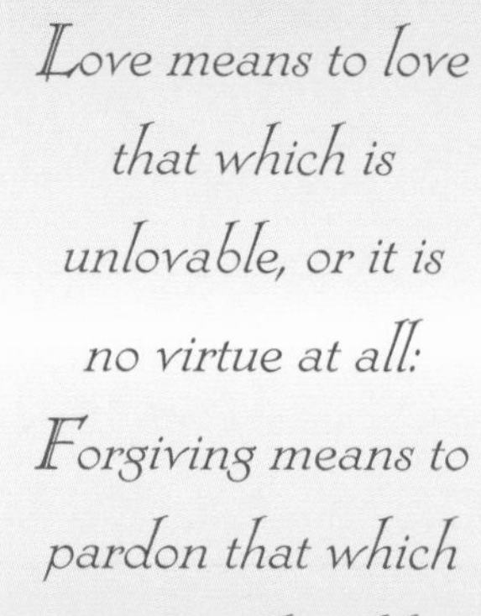


Then his faith rallied. Ashamed of himself, he ran and threw his arms around the leper's neck, kissed him, and passed on. A moment later he turned back, thinking that he might call a word of encouragement to the leper. But he saw no one—only the empty path stretching toward the horizon in the hot sunlight. For the rest of his life, Francis was convinced that he had not met a leper, but Christ Himself.

To love the unlovable truly requires God's divine, unconditional love—a love He promises to us when we ask Him for this gracious gift.

*Be gentle* and *forbearing with one another and, if one has a difference (a grievance or complaint) against another, readily pardoning each other; even as the Lord has [freely] forgiven you, so must you also [forgive].*
COLOSSIANS 3:13 AMP

*If the husband and wife can possibly afford it, they should definitely have separate bathrooms for the sake of their marriage.*

Grammy-award-winning singer, Anita Baker, recently said that one of the secrets to her happy marriage was this: "My husband and I don't hassle each other. . . . I've been very careful to allow him to have his own life, apart from me, and I don't get into his business. If he wants advice, I'll wait for him to ask. If he wants to talk, I try to listen to him instead of telling him, 'Well, if it were my business'. . . . The only thing I will do in terms of involving myself is tell him when it's five o'clock. If he continues working, then I know he needs to.

"As a real estate developer, he's very successful, and I'm really proud of him. I just try to let him have his space and he definitely lets me have mine. So when we come together, it's exciting. I have stuff to talk to him about, he's got stuff to talk to me about and we definitely have the kids in common. We give each other room to have a life outside of each other."

Giving a spouse "space" in a relationship may not mean separate bathrooms, but each person in a relationship definitely needs room, activities, responsibilities, and dreams to call their own.

*A happy heart is good medicine* and
*a cheerful mind works healing.*
PROVERBS 17:22 AMP

A successful marriage is a give-and-take relationship, with each party doing 90 percent giving and only ten percent taking!

Here are ten questions to ask yourself about your ability to give and take:

1. Are you willing to give silence when your spouse needs a little quiet time?
2. Are you willing to take a rebuke and let it rest unchallenged?
3. Are you willing to give your spouse the benefit of the doubt?

*A good husband should be deaf and a good wife should be blind.*

4. Are you willing to take on the extra chore during a time when you know your spouse is stressed out?
5. Are you willing to give a word of spontaneous encouragement?

6. Are you willing to take time to spend with your spouse—alone, and without interruption?
7. Are you willing to give your spouse the courtesy of "please" and "thank you"?
8. Are you willing to take a 'time out' when a disagreement appears to be overheating?
9. Are you willing to give a compliment?
10. Are you willing to take criticism?

*Be gentle and ready to forgive;*
*never hold grudges.*
COLOSSIANS 3:13 TLB

*Everyone has an invisible sign hanging from his neck saying, "Make me feel important!"*

A teacher once asked her group of kindergarteners to answer the question, "What is love?"

One little girl piped up, "Love is when your mommy reads you a bedtime story."

Another little girl quickly added, "And real love is when she doesn't skip a-n-y pages."

Every person needs to feel that they are truly acknowledged and made to feel important. But we also need to know this need for recognition is *received* in different ways. What one person may receive as an expression of approval and appreciation may not be received in the same way by another person. Find out what is meaningful to *your* spouse. For some, an expression of importance may be the amount of time spent with your spouse, or special care given to details. In other cases, your spouse may experience great encouragement from words of praise or gifts of appreciation. In yet other cases, your spouse may feel more important when you go the second mile or do chores that by agreement aren't your own.

Find a way to make your loved one feel "extra special" today.

*Therefore encourage one another and build each other up, just as in fact you are doing.*
I THESSALONIANS 5:11 NIV

Joanne grew up in a family where relatives freely came and went in each others' homes. They even rummaged through the refrigerator and used the phone without asking. Paul, on the other hand, grew up in a home and neighborhood where each family kept very much to itself. Such behavior would have been unthinkable to his family. You can imagine how appalled Paul was when walking into his kitchen one morning to find Joanne's nephew searching through the cupboards for an unopened box of cereal! For her part, Joanne just couldn't understand why she had to extend a "formal" invitation before Paul's parents would stop by to visit their grandchildren.

*A thick skin is a gift from God.*

Through the years, Paul and Joanne have adjusted. Paul is still uncomfortable with what seems like continual drop-in company, but he has chosen not to let it interfere with his relationship with Joanne. He just shrugs his shoulders and laughs. Joanne has made it a point to call her in-laws with greater frequency and invite them to their home.

"But mostly," Joanne has said, "we both toughened up a little and decided not to let little differences become big."

*A man's wisdom gives him patience,*
*it is to his glory to overlook an offense.*
PROVERBS 19:11 NIV

# *All things are difficult before they are easy.*

Convenience is not only a popular word today, it has become something we expect out of life. Convenience, however, is a word that should be applied to things, not people. We may have modern "conveniences" such as microwave ovens, no-frost refrigerators, and supersonic airplanes. We may even have "convenience stores." But we should never have a convenient friend, co-worker, or spouse. And never should we value a relationship only because it is convenient. When things get tough, the first things to go are the conveniences in life. Things may be disposable, but relationships should never be.

A man once overheard a young couple rehearsing wedding vows they had composed themselves. They pledged "to stay with you for as long as I love you." The man asked them after the rehearsal, "How long do you think that will be?" Neither had an answer.

Convenience says, "I'll stand by you—if it suits my schedule, fits in with my current priorities, or seems to suit my mood at the moment." Commitment, in contrast to convenience, proclaims, "I'll be with you through thick and thin. I'll be there when you need me, in spite of my schedule, agenda, or emotions."

*Blessed is the man who perseveres under trial, because when he has stood the test, he will receive the crown of life that God has promised to those who love him.*

JAMES 1:12 NIV

Paul McElroy writes eloquently in *Quiet Thoughts,* "Marriage is the bond that ties two loving hearts together. As each ministers to the other, stands by the other, complements as well as compliments the other, the relationship is made fast like the strands of a rope. Love does not consist of two people gazing fondly into each other's eyes, but in moving together in the same direction. As the maple cannot grow under the shadow of the towering oak, so one helpmate cannot develop under the domination of the other. Husband and wife, like two musicians playing different notes on different instruments, should be able to create harmony as the tones of one blend with those of the other."

*Marriage is like harmony: two sets of notes for the same song.*

A couple was honored with a party on their 60th wedding anniversary. The husband, known for being very shy, was asked to share the secret of their long marriage. Unable to speak, he reached for a nearby fiddle and began to play. His wife picked up the tune and began to sing in her still-steady and clear soprano voice. When the song ended, the wife said simply, "We both know all the same songs—we just express them in our own ways. But I never sing for any other fiddler, and he never plays for any other singer."

*Complete my joy by being of the same mind, having the same love, being in full accord and of one mind.*
PHILIPPIANS 2:2 RSV

*Intimacy is the mystical bond of friendship, commitment, and understanding.*

Shortly after his wife died of cancer, a man found a note written by his wife—apparently a list of qualities she wanted her husband to know she appreciated. She wrote:

Loved. Cared. Worried.
Helped me when I was sick.
Forgave me for a lot of things.
Stood by me.
Always complimentary.
Provided everything I ever needed.
Warmth. Humor. Kindness.
Thoughtfulness.
Always there when I needed you.
Good friend.

Although the woman probably intended her list to be part of her husband's thank-you letter for their nearly four decades of marriage, she also gave to the world a good prescription for marriage!

A man once asked, "How do I know if I have what it takes to stand by my wife if she were to be injured or become seriously ill?"

A friend who had lived through such an experience responded, "If you love her enough, you won't even ask the question at the time it happens."

*There is a friend who sticks*
*closer than a brother.*
PROVERBS 18:24 AMP

There's very little that is subtle about love, although we like to think of love in soft, gentle terms.

We may say we have "fallen" in love, but in fact, love plummets into our hearts. It seems to come from nowhere. One day we feel very little, or nothing. The next day, we feel love throbbing in us, as if injected into us full strength, without warning.

*If love is a jigsaw puzzle, falling in love is finding the corners.*

We may say we are "growing together" in love. In fact, our love causes us to collide together as if we were two planets on an overlapping orbit.

We like to speak of the "mystery" of love. But in fact, love is the most real, obvious, and overwhelming emotion any of us will ever feel.

We speak of the lyrical language of love. But most of us are tongue-tied by it and stand silently in awe of it.

We may say we are warmed slowly by love's embrace. But in fact, love usually erupts within us like a volcano, then flows over us so as to incapacitate us from feeling any other emotion.

We may think of love as being fragile, to be tended with gentleness. In fact, love is the strongest thing we can ever know—it alone has the power to endure and to remain . . . *forever.*

*But now abide faith, hope, love,*
*these three; but the greatest of these is love.*
I CORINTHIANS 13:13 NAS

## *If you would be wealthy, think of saving as well as getting.*

Keith Nicholson won $426,495 in a soccer pool in the early 1960s. In commenting on their winnings, his wife announced that they were going to "spend, spend, spend."

And spend they did! They purchased a luxury home for $47,600 and moved out of their low-rent city housing apartment—leaving behind most of their friends and family. And they gave parties almost every night. In four years, they managed to spend $196,000. Later Mrs. Nicholson said, "We had oodles of money but we lost our friends. The people we had known in the old days, whom we really wanted to see, never came along."

Then in 1966, Keith was killed in an automobile accident. The $5,600 car he had purchased from his winnings was totaled. After his death, $107,113 went to the government in death taxes. The remainder was invested, half in trust for the Nicholson's three children, and half for Mrs. Nicholson. Her income from the trust fund—all that remained from the jackpot winnings—was $25 a week.

Having money doesn't only refer to what you have available to spend, but what you have available because you choose *not* to spend it.

*The ants are a people not strong, yet they lay up their food in the summer.*
PROVERBS 30:25 AMP

*Dad to Jimmy when Jimmy was born:* "Son, I'm going to make sure you never have a care in the world. I'm going to work to give you the best life has to offer."

*Dad to Jimmy when Jimmy was five:* "Sorry, I can't be there for your first day of school, son, but you'll do fine. I should be home by the weekend."

*Dad to Jimmy when Jimmy was ten:* "You'll like camp. Just remember—don't do anything I wouldn't do. See you in two months."

*Dad to Jimmy when Jimmy was eighteen:* "Write when you get there, son. I know you'll do just fine in college. Drop us a line occasionally."

No one on his deathbed ever said "I wish I had spent more time on my business."

*Dad to Jimmy when Jimmy was arrested at age twenty-five for drug possession:* "Why?

What happened? Where did I go wrong, son? I gave you everything."

*Jimmy to Dad:* "Except the one thing I wanted, Dad."

*Dad:* "What was that? You had a car, a college education, a nice home, everything you could need. I gave you the best of everything. What more could you have wanted?"

*Jimmy:* "You, Dad."

*"Do not labor for the food which perishes, but for the food which endures to eternal life."*
JOHN 6:27 RSV

*May the love you share be as timeless as the tides and as deep as the sea.*

A good relationship has a pattern like a dance and is built on some of the same rules. The partners do not need to hold on tightly, because they move confidently in the same pattern, intricate . . . swift and free, like a country dance of Mozart's. To touch heavily would be to arrest the pattern and freeze the movement. There is no place here for the possessive clutch, the clinging arm, the heavy hand; only the slightest touch in passing. Now arm in arm, fact to face, back to back—it does not matter which. They know they are partners moving to the same rhythm, creating a pattern together, being invisibly nourished by it. . . .

When the heart is flooded with love there is no room in it for fear, doubt, or hesitation. It is this lack of fear that makes for the dance. When each partner loves so completely that he has forgotten to ask himself whether or not he is loved in return; when he only knows he loves and is moving to its music—then, and then only, are two people able to dance perfectly in tune to the same rhythm.

—Anne Morrow Lindberg
*Gift From the Sea*

*Love never ends.*
I Corinthians 13:8 RSV

Someone once noted these eight reasons for a woman to buy an item: because her husband said she couldn't have it; it made her look thin; it came from Paris; the neighbors couldn't afford it; no one else had it; everyone had it; it was different; and just because.

*My wife is very punctual. In fact, she buys everything on time.*

Consider the example, however, of Bill Hughes, a shipyard worker. London tax officials thought they could prove Hughes was involved in illegal activity when they found he had a savings account of $16,800, yet earned only $56 a week. Instead, Hughes told them his "secrets:" He never ate candy, smoked, drank, or went out with women. He shaved with his brother's razor blades, charged his grandmother 12 percent interest on money she borrowed from him, worked a night shift, and wore his father's shoes to save on shoe leather. He also went thirteen years without buying a new suit, never bought a single flower, only saw one movie in his entire life, ate everything served to him at mealtimes even if he didn't want it, and patched everything he owned until the patches wouldn't hold (including his underwear). Finally, Bill never took a holiday trip that cost more than 56 cents in fares and fees.

There is a balance to be found between spending too much and spending too little!

*The heart of her husband doth safely trust in her, so that he shall have no need of spoil.*

PROVERBS 31:11 KJV

*God gave women a sense of humor—so they could understand their husband's bad jokes.*

What some women have to contend with! Consider the wife of a hard-to-please husband who was determined to try to satisfy him. "What would you like for breakfast this morning, dear?" she asked sweetly.

"Coffee and toast, grits and sausage, and two eggs—one fried, one scrambled," he grumbled. She immediately began cooking then set before him the meal he requested. Rather than offer her any compliment, however, the man took one look at the plate and said, "I should have expected it. You scrambled the wrong egg."

Or consider the woman who went out for a walk with her husband one afternoon and met friends on their walk. The husband invited the couple back to their house for supper. The wife, too, encouraged them to come, but asked that they wait ten minutes before heading over. She then whispered to her husband, "I'm going to rush over to the deli for a few things. You go home and straighten up." When she returned from her record-setting trip to the deli, she found everything in their home just as they had left it—newspapers strewn about and dishes still in the living room. Her husband was "straightening" the house by changing the light bulb on the back porch!

*Husbands, love your wives, just as Christ also loved the church.*
EPHESIANS 5:25 NAS

Many of us think of "springs" as emerging only high in the mountains or as bubbling up in an arid desert to create an oasis.

Some springs emerge from the earth very close to saltwater seas. The water gushes up there from the beach sands just as sweet as any that might burst from the rocks in the high hills. When the sea is at low tide, one can dig into the spring and drink from its clear, refreshing water.

*Lean on each other's strengths; forgive each other's weaknesses.*

Once the tide rolls back in and covers the spring, one might assume it would "pollute" the spring and cause it to become salty. Not so. When the tide again is low, the spring continues to produce fresh, sparkling water, just as sweet as before.

So, too, is it with forgiveness born of love. No wrong, cruelty, or rejection can have an impact on genuine forgiveness. We forgive "no matter what"—first, because it is the nature of love to forgive. Second, because it is our forgiveness that has the greatest potential to impact the heart of those who wrong us. This is true even if we see no evidence of that during our lifetime.

And finally it is forgiveness that keeps our own souls fresh and clear and sparkling. If we allow the brackish waters of unforgiveness to enter us, we become victims of evil, not overcomers of it.

*Bearing with one another,*
*and forgiving one another.*
COLOSSIANS 3:13 NKJV

# *Never, never, be too proud to say "I'm sorry" to your child when you've made a mistake.*

Jerry was part of a basketball program in which every boy was allowed to play, no matter his skill. His parents, however, were mortified the first time they saw him play. They insisted that he quit and give himself to something in which he might succeed.

Not long after, Jerry's coach called to see what had happened. Jerry's dad said, "I hated to see him embarrass himself."

The coach replied, "I don't think Jerry was embarrassed. Were *you?*"

Jerry's dad was big enough to say, "Yeah, I guess I was. Sports were easy for me."

The coach advised, "Work with your son. Teach him what you know. But please don't take the fun out of the game for him."

When Jerry's dad asked him if he wanted to play, Jerry replied, "More than anything!" So his dad apologized. Then they began shooting baskets together. The more they played together, the more Jerry's game began to improve. But most of all, Jerry's dad imparted to him staying power, an enduring ability to face up to difficulties and overcome them. As a result, in just two years, Jerry was shooting baskets from anywhere in the court!

Practice and encouragement often work where criticism fails.

*Fathers, do not irritate* and *provoke your children to anger [do not exasperate them to resentment], but rear them [tenderly] in the discipline and the counsel of the Lord.*
EPHESIANS 6:4 AMP

A parent once said to his teenage son as he left the house: "Now don't take the car anywhere." What do you suppose happened? The son not only took the car for a spin, but wrapped it around a nearby lamp post!

A teacher once told her class, "I'm leaving the room for just a few minutes. Sit quietly in your seats and work on your assignment until I return." What happened? Why, of course . . . the class was in an uproar when she returned five minutes later.

*Friendships, like marriages, are dependent on avoiding the unforgivable.*

What is the one deed for which you would have the most difficulty forgiving your spouse?

What is the one behavior you find most despicable?

What is the one situation you never hope to experience in your life?

What is the character trait you most despise?

What is the most annoying habit you can imagine another person having?

The more you discuss those things with your spouse, the more you bring them to mind, the more readily they can become . . . temptations. Steer clear of what you *don't* want to have happen in your life—even in your conversation.

*Be kind and compassionate to*
*one another, forgiving each other,*
*just as in Christ God forgave you.*
EPHESIANS 4:32 NIV

*You cannot show a kindness too soon because you never know how soon it will be too late!*

Most of us make "gift lists" at Christmas time, but true Christianity is manifested in a continual giving from the heart. Make each day a day to give a gift. Consider putting some of these things on your gift list:

Write a long overdue note to a friend.

Hug someone tightly and whisper, "I love you."

Sit down on the floor and play with a child.

Seek to mend a broken relationship.

Take a walk with a friend.

Turn off the television and talk to your family.

Treat someone to an ice cream cone.

Take out the trash without being asked.

Visit an older person.

Offer to babysit for a weary mother.

Praise a trait you admire in a co-worker.

Send a contribution to the charity of your choice.

Bake a pie for a homebound neighbor.

Write a thank-you note to your child's teacher.

Call a family member who lives out of state.

Pray for the ministers of your church.

Fix a candlelight dinner for your spouse.

*This kind of giving never breaks or goes out of style!*

*But encourage one another day after day,*
*as long as it is* still *called "Today."*
HEBREWS 3:13 NAS

Prayer sometimes changes things. More frequently, however, prayer seems to change the person who prays. In the case of King Hezekiah, prayer changed things. God told Hezekiah that the time had come for him to die. But Hezekiah prayed that God would extend his life and God gave him fifteen more years to live. (See 2 Kings 20:1-11.)

*Daily prayers will diminish your cares.*

In the Apostle Paul's case, prayer did *not* change things. Paul prayed three times for an affliction, but his condition remained the same. Paul's attitude, however, changed toward the "thorn" in his flesh as he discovered new insight into the sufficiency of God's grace. (See 2 Corinthians 12:7-9.)

We are basically selfish; therefore our prayer requests are often selfish. We desire God to change His plans for our benefit. What we must recognize is that while God does not promise us a problem-free life, He does promise to walk through our problems with us. And if we will allow Him to do so, He will transform us ever more into the likeness of His Son Jesus Christ. Sometimes situations do need to change, but very often it is our own heart that needs changing.

The *cause* of our worry is not the real problem from God's perspective—rather, it is that we worry.

*Have no anxiety about anything,*
*but in everything by prayer and*
*supplication with thanksgiving let*
*your requests be made known to God.*
PHILIPPIANS 4:6 RSV

*It is more important to get in the first thought than the last word.*

Virtually every problem that frustrates or angers us . . . *has a solution!* We can usually find that solution if we'll only put our emotions on hold for awhile and consider the situation from another point of view.

Lance came home from work angry that one of his best supervisors had quit to take a better-paying job. He had put a great deal of time and energy into training this woman. Once he calmed his emotions, however, he began to think, *How would I feel if I were in her shoes—liking my present job but offered a better-paying one?* The next morning, Lance talked to his manager about offering the woman a small raise and a shift in her hours so she might be home when her children arrived from school. The manager agreed, and the supervisor quickly accepted the offer.

Diane became frustrated that her sons' toys seemed to be continually strewn about their room. Tired of scolding them, she calmed herself and thought, *What could I do to make picking up easier?* The next day she bought an inexpensive stack of storage containers, a preprinted chart, and a stop-watch. She made picking-up a game the boys loved.

What bothers you today? Rather than explode, stop to think, *What might I do to change things?*

*Let every one be quick to hear,*
*slow to speak* and *slow to anger.*
JAMES 1:19 NAS

Most of us have heard the old saying, "Women give sex in order to get intimacy. Men give intimacy in order to get sex." We laugh at the play on words, but in truth, men and women seem to want different things from a sexual relationship. One national survey recently showed that 72 percent of the women polled would choose loving closeness and tenderness to sex if they could have only one or the other.

*A husband should compliment his wife, bring her flowers and tell her that he cares. These are the ingredients of genuine passion.*

For many men, sex is a matter of primal conquest—of getting what the man needs to meet a physical drive. That drive is rooted largely in what a man sees and senses. For women, sex is a part of romance—of having dreams fulfilled. A woman's approach to sex is based largely in her mind.

To truly satisfy a partner, each must recognize these differences. A woman is wise to make herself as attractive to her husband as possible. A man is wise to trigger his wife's imagination with genuine compliments and expressions of tender care.

Marriage is a matter of meeting each other's needs, and very often, understanding of those needs must come before a spouse can begin to meet them!

*Her children rise up and bless her;*
*Her husband* also, *and he praises her,*
saying: *"Many daughters have done*
*nobly, But you excel them all."*
PROVERBS 31:28,29 NAS

*Before criticizing your wife's faults, you must remember it may have been these very defects which prevented her from getting a better husband than the one she married.*

A six-year-old boy was sent home one day with a note from his teacher. The note suggested that the boy be taken out of school sine he was "too stupid to learn." The boy was Thomas A. Edison.

A grandfather once gave his grandson ten shillings for writing a eulogy about his grandmother. The grandfather said as he gave him the money, "There, that is the first money you ever earned for your poetry, and take my word for it, it will be the last." The lad was Alfred Tennyson.

A woman once hesitated in letting her daughter marry a printer who had asked for her hand in marriage. She was concerned that the United States already had two printing offices, and she feared the nation might not be able to support a third. The printer was Benjamin Franklin.

So often we fail to recognize the greatness in those with whom we live. It's almost as if we can't see the full length and breadth of the person's life because we are standing too close to him or her. Be careful who you criticize. You may very well be putting down someone whose name will go down in history, even if yours will not.

*Therefore let us not judge one another anymore, but rather determine this—not to put an obstacle or a stumbling block in a brother's way.*

ROMANS 14:13 NAS

Johnny lived in the South Pacific, where all the islanders spoke highly of him. Yet, when it came time for him to find a wife, the people shook their heads in disbelief. The normal custom was for a man to obtain a wife by paying her father in cattle. Four to six cows was considered a high price. Johnny chose a plain, skinny young woman who walked with her shoulders hunched over and her head down. And she was very shy. But Johnny offered her father eight cows for her!

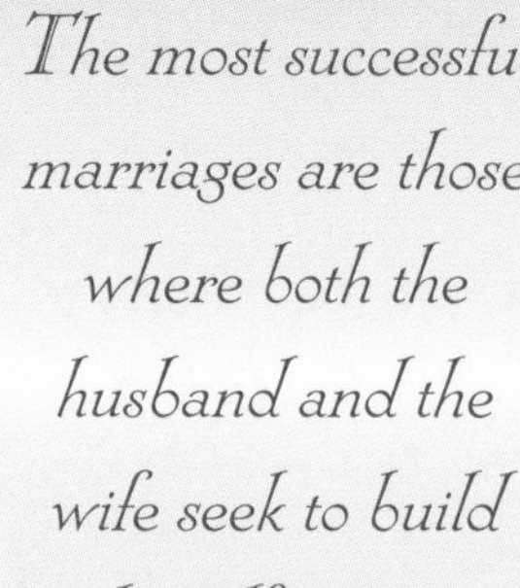


People laughed at Johnny, thinking her father had scored a major victory.

A visitor arrived in Johnny's village several months later and heard the story of Johnny's eight-cow wife. When he saw Johnny and met his wife, the visitor was extremely surprised. He didn't see a shy, plain, hesitant woman, but rather, a very beautiful, poised, and confident woman. When Johnny saw the visitor's surprise, he said, "I wanted an eight-cow woman. When I paid eight cows for her and began to treat her like an eight-cow woman, she began to believe in herself as an eight-cow woman. She discovered she was worth more than any other woman on the islands. What matters most is what a woman thinks about herself."

*Therefore encourage one another,*
*and build up one another.*
I THESSALONIANS 5:11 NAS

*Our children are watching us live, and what we are shouts louder than anything we say.*

Karl grew up in Germany as a young Jewish boy whose life was deeply rooted in the acts of piety and devotion related to the family's religion. He had a deep respect for his father, who was zealous in attending synagogue services and studying the Torah.

When Karl was a teenager, the family moved to another town in Germany which had no synagogue. So Karl's father announced to the family that they were going to abandon their Jewish traditions and join the Lutheran church, the church to which all the important people in the city belonged. The family was stunned, but the father gave them no explanation. Karl was especially bewildered and disappointed and eventually became very bitter over what had happened. He left Germany and went to England to study. There he began to compose a book to reflect the new ideas he was encountering. In it he described religion as an "opiate for the masses" that could be explained totally in terms of economics.

For nearly a century, more than a billion people lived under the system advocated by a disillusioned, bitter Karl Marx. The influence of his father's hypocrisy reached around the world.

*Let us not love with word or with tongue, but in deed and truth.*
I JOHN 3:18 NAS

At the height of the segregation storm in the United States, a six-year-old girl headed out for her first day of school. Her elementary school was one that had been integrated recently and tension still seemed to exist in the community. Her mother met her anxiously at the door, eager to hear how the day had gone. "Did everything go all right, honey?" she asked.

"Oh, Mother! You know what?" the little girl said eagerly. "A little black girl sat next to me."

*The sunlight of love will kill all the germs of jealousy and hate.*

With growing apprehension the mother asked, "And what happened?"

The little girl replied, "We were both so scared about our first day at school that we held hands all day."

Very often our jealousy and hate are born out of a lack of information—we simply don't know a person or an individual member of a group. Once we discover the many things that we share in common with another person—including our fears, our hopes, our concerns, our desires—the things that comprise our differences seem to pale into the background.

Love grows when we allow one another our unique differences.

*Love never fails.*

I CORINTHIANS 13:8 NAS

## *Stack every bit of criticism between two layers of praise.*

In *How to Change Your Spouse,* Norman Wright tells about an incident that happened early in his marriage: "I was fairly sloppy when it came to hanging up my pajamas in the morning. I took care of most of my other clothes, but in the morning when I took off my PJ's, I gave them a fling toward a hook in the closet . . . or else they stayed on the bed. I was reminded about it numerous times and I'd give verbal assent, but somehow the message never took hold.

"One day when I was seated on the couch reading the newspaper, Joyce sat down next to me and waited until I turned toward her. I noticed that my pajamas were neatly folded on her lap. She put her arm around me, looked me in the eye and said, 'Norm, I just know that a man of your organizational ability and your attention to detail and results would have such a sense of satisfaction going to work each day knowing that your pajamas were hanging neatly on the closet hook. Thank you for listening.' And with that she walked out of the room leaving me with my mouth hanging open. I didn't realize until a couple of months later, that since that day, I had been hanging up my pajamas."

*Correct, rebuke and encourage—with great patience and careful instruction.*
2 TIMOTHY 4:2 NIV

A group of girls were gathered together one rainy afternoon. One of them opened the door for a moment, and as she did, a wave of aroma—the sweet scent of wet, green, growing plants—filled the room.

*Of all the home remedies, a good wife is best.*

The girl at the door turned and said to her friends, "Can you smell the sweetbrier down by the gate?" The girls nodded. She added, "It's always fragrant, but never so fragrant as when it rains."

Then one of the girls in the room said impulsively, "It reminds me of my aunt." The other girls giggled slightly and one asked, "Why would you say that?"

The girl explained, "So many flowers are fragrant—just look, this garden has dozens of rose bushes, and their roses are sweet-smelling. But the sweetbrier is the only other plant with fragrant leaves. Everything my aunt does—not just the large things, but the common everyday things—including the leaves as well as the blossoms—has something beautiful in it. There is a gentleness in her spirit, a thoughtfulness, a graciousness that goes out in everything she does and in every word she speaks."

A spouse who makes each small moment in life special, helps all of life to take on a new wonder.

*He who finds a wife finds a good thing,*
*And obtains favor from the Lord.*
PROVERBS 18:22 NKJV

# *A woman must be a genius to create a good husband.*

In *A Time for Remembering,* Ruth Bell Graham writes that when she was a teenager, leaving her childhood home in China for schooling in Korea, she fully intended to be an old maid missionary to Tibet. She did, however, give some thought to the particulars she would require in a man *if* she could ever be persuaded to marry. She wrote in her diary:

"If I marry: He must be so tall that when he is on his knees, as one has said, he reaches all the way to heaven. His shoulders must be broad enough to bear the burden of a family. His lips must be strong enough to smile, firm enough to say no, and tender enough to kiss. Love must be so deep that it takes its stand in Christ and so wide that it takes the whole lost world in. He must be active enough to save souls. He must be big enough to be gentle and great enough to be thoughtful. His arms must be strong enough to carry a little child."

Did Ruth Bell find such a man in Billy Graham? Perhaps not on the day she met him, as much as on the day they celebrated their fiftieth wedding anniversary.

*She opens her mouth in skillful and godly Wisdom, and on her tongue is the law of kindness.*
PROVERBS 31:26 AMP

Many women today are weary of trying to be "superwoman"—super mom, super wife, a super professional on the job, a perfect woman. They are coming to the realization that a woman may be able to "have it all," but probably not all at the same time! Men, too, are struggling with a "must be perfect" syndrome that seems to pervade our culture.

*Success in marriage is more than finding the right person. It's also a matter of being the right person.*

Rather than try to live up to the world's definition of success, we are wise to discover what it means to be successful in God's eyes, which is being the person *He* created you to be.

This does not mean we should settle for second best in our lives, or fail to develop our talents. We are always to pursue our potential and to seek to grow in our faith. What it *does* mean is that we are free to pursue what it is the Lord calls and directs us to do at any point in our lives. And to express ourselves in unique and creative ways.

A woman named Kate had this perspective when she answered a reporter who asked her about her life: "I've had nine jobs: waitress, clerk, personnel manager, student, nurse, wife, mom, nursing administrator, and teacher in a nursing school. But I've had only one personality: Kate."

*"And just as you want people to treat you, treat them in the same way."*
LUKE 6:31 NAS

*Unless loving your family is a high priority, you may gain the world and lose your children.*

A little girl was put to bed in a dark room. She heartily disliked being alone, so her mother brought her favorite doll named Happy to cuddle as she lay in the dark. But the girl still cried and begged her mother to stay in the room with her. So the mother patiently reminded her daughter that she had both Happy and God in the room with her, and that she need not feel lonely or afraid.

The little girl listened, but after her mother left, she began to sob again. The mother returned to her room and said in a sterner tone of voice, "Honey, you aren't alone. You have Happy and God with you."

The little girl sobbed, "But Mother, I want someone who can hug me back."

As strong as our faith may be, and as noble as our words may be to our children, our children still need to *feel* our presence. They need quality and quantity time. They need to know we are available to hug them, when and where *they* feel the need for those hugs.

The Father certainly is with us always, but Jesus put our role in perspective when He said, "As the Father hath sent me, so send I you." Your role as a parent is the most important thing you will ever do.

*Perfect love casts out fear.*

I John 4:18 NAS

*I shouted aloud and louder*
*While out on the plain one day;*
*The sound grew faint and fainter*
*Until it had died away.*
*My words had gone forever,*
*They left no trace or track,*
*But the hills nearby caught up the cry*
*And sent an echo back.*

*I spoke a word in anger*
*To one who was my friend,*
*Like a knife it cut him deeply,*
*A wound that was hard to mend.*
*That word, so thoughtlessly uttered,*
*I would we could both forget,*
*But its echo lives and memory gives*

The world needs more warm hearts and fewer hot heads.

*The recollection yet.*

*How many hearts are broken,*
*How many friends are lost*
*By some unkind word spoken*
*Before we count the cost!*
*But a word or deed of kindness*
*Will repay a hundredfold,*
*For it echoes again in the hearts of men*
*And carries a joy untold.*

—C. A. Lufburrow

*Good sense makes a man slow to anger,*
*and it is his glory to overlook an offense.*
PROVERBS 19:11 RSV

*A torn jacket is soon mended; but hard words bruise the heart of a child.*

A banker was appalled when his awkward teenage son began wearing ragged clothing and an earring in his ear. His first impulse was to demand that his son "shape up and clean up." But before he said anything, he thought, *My son must feel that he isn't a part of the school crowd. He's dressing this way to feel accepted. Rather than work on his dress code, I need to work on his esteem.*

So a few weeks later, the father invited his son to go with him to his annual banker's club banquet. The two had a great time. Even though the son sported a streak of orange in his hair, he wore a suit to the event and behaved superbly, recalling the names of his father's friends and conversing confidently with them. He had responded to the unspoken message of his father's invitation: "Son, I'm proud of you."

Criticism wounds and tears down. Praise heals and builds up. Your child will encounter plenty of criticism in his or her life, without any of it coming from you. Part of "raising" a child is to literally raise their self-esteem and sights to new horizons and to raise their level of faith. That kind of raising is the product of praising.

*"But I tell you that men will have to give account on the day of judgment for every careless word they have spoken."*

MATTHEW 12:36 NIV

In an article in the *Los Angeles Times,* Ann Wells wrote: "My brother-in-law opened the bottom drawer of my sister's bureau and lifted out a tissue-wrapped package . . . He discarded the tissue and handed me the slip. It was exquisite; silk, hand-made and trimmed with a cobweb of lace. The price tag with an astronomical figure on it was still attached.

*You have a lifetime to enjoy one another. Don't waste a day of it.*

"'Jan bought this the first time we went to New York, at least eight or nine years ago. She never wore it. She was saving it for a special occasion. Well, I guess this is the occasion.'

"He took the slip from me and put it on the bed with the other clothes we were taking to the mortician. His hands lingered on the soft material for a moment, then he slammed the drawer shut and turned to me.

"Don't ever save anything for a special occasion. Every day you are alive is a special occasion.'

"I'm still thinking about his words, and they've changed my life. . . . I'm not 'saving' anything; we use our good china and crystal for every special event—such as losing a pound, getting the sink unstopped, the first camellia blossom. . . . "

*Make today as special as it is!*

*Live happily with the woman you love*
*through the fleeting days of life.*
ECCLESIASTES 9:9 TLB

# *Children need love, especially when they do not deserve it.*

This recipe for child-raising is one that has truly stood the test of time and brings a "sweet taste" to the mouth of every child who partakes of it!

*Recipe for Child-Raising*
(from *The Living Bible)*

1 cup of Proverbs 22:6

2 Tablespoons of Proverbs 19:18

1 Dash of Proverbs 23:13

1 Teaspoon of Proverbs 3:5

½ cup of Titus 2:3,5,6

Add a pinch of Ephesians 6:4

Mix all the ingredients, add a pound of persistence, one cup of love, and stir until right consistency. This recipe is recommended by the Creator of Mankind as suitable for all children!

Proverbs 22:6—Teach a child to choose the right path, and when he is older he will remain upon it.

Proverbs 19:18—Discipline your son in his early years while there is hope. If you don't you will ruin his life.

Proverbs 23:13—Don't fail to correct your children.

Proverbs 3:5—Trust the Lord completely.

Titus 2:3,5,6—The older women must train the younger women to live quietly, to love their husbands and their children, and to be sensible and clean minded, spending their time in their own homes, being kind and obedient to their husbands. Urge the young men to behave carefully, taking life seriously.

Ephesians 6:4—Don't keep on scolding and nagging your children, making them angry and resentful. Rather, bring them up with the loving discipline the Lord himself approves, with suggestions and godly advice.

*"Let the children come to me, and do not hinder them, for the kingdom of heaven belongs to such as these."*

MATTHEW 19:14 NIV

A teacher decided to honor each of her seniors using a method developed by Helice Bridges of Del Mar, California. She called each student to the front of the class, told the entire class how the student had made a difference to her and the class, then presented him or her with a blue ribbon imprinted with gold letters: "Who I Am Makes A Difference."

*Loving can cost a lot, but not loving always costs more.*

After the ceremony, the teacher gave three identical ribbons to each student and instructed them to go out and spread the acknowledgement ceremony in the community. One of the boys went to a junior executive in a nearby company and honored him for helping with a project. He gave the junior exec the two extra ribbons so he might honor someone who had impacted his life. The junior exec gave his boss a ribbon and the extra ribbon to pass on.

That night, the boss went home and told his 14-year-old son what had happened. Then he took out the extra ribbon and said, "As I was driving home tonight, I started thinking about whom I would honor with this ribbon, and I thought about you. You're a great kid and I love you."

The boy began to cry as he said, "I was planning on committing suicide tomorrow, Dad, because I didn't think you loved me. Now I don't need to."

*And if I give all my possessions to feed* the poor,
*and if I deliver my body to be burned, but*
*do not have love, it profits me nothing.*
I CORINTHIANS 13:3 NAS

*In trying times,*
*don't quit trying.*

Take any major individual-oriented athletic event, and you'll probably find that far more people are starters than are finishers. How many people have started the Tour de France bicycle race, the Boston Marathon, or a swim of the English Channel . . . only to drop out before reaching their goal?

Those who finish these long-distance endurance events speak of "pushing through the wall." The "wall" in these events is the point where the body cries out to the mind, "We can't go on. I've given all I can. I don't have any more to give." Every endurance racer hits this wall, including those who are in top shape and those who may have completed the event in years past. Those who push through the wall are those whose *mind* says back to their *body,* "Oh yes we can." The mind compels—yes, forces—the body to keep moving.

This ability to keep moving when your instincts say otherwise is called *perseverance.* Every couple needs to keep that word in mind when they hit the wall in their relationship. Perseverance is the ability to hang on, rather than hang up. It's the ability to keep going, rather than to call it quits. It's a matter of the heart saying to the relationship, "Oh yes, we can."

*And let us not grow weary*
*in well-doing, for in due season*
*we shall reap, if we do not lose heart.*
GALATIANS 6:9 RSV

Too many marriages are rooted in passion. But to grow in depth, a marriage must not only be a "love affair," but a deep and growing friendship—a meeting not only of bodies, but of minds, hearts, and souls.

*Friendship is the marriage of the soul.*

How special it is when a spouse says, "I married my best friend." Even more special is the spouse who says after many years of marriage, "I am married to my best friend!"

*I love you not only for what you are, but for what I am when I am with you;*

*I love you not only for what you have made of yourself, but for what you are making of me;*

*I love you not for closing your ears to the discords in me, but for adding to the music in me by worshipful listening;*

*You have done it without a touch, without a word, without a sign. You have done it just by being yourself.*

*Perhaps that is what being a friend means, after all.*

—Author Unknown

*Two are better than one, because*
*they have a good return for their work.*
ECCLESIASTES 4:9 NIV

# *People in love want what's best for each other.*

A man who had once worked as a general contractor for a large development company suddenly found himself the victim of "downsizing." He quickly put out his resumés, but without success. For the next year, he painted the house, carpooled the children, did the grocery shopping, and generally felt miserable and depressed. As the crisis reverberated through the family, his wife continued to work full-time as a teacher. But her salary alone couldn't support the family. Their savings became sorely depleted. Then the grades of their teenage son began to drop dramatically, and the mother insisted the family enter counseling. She said, "I insisted the counseling was for me, although it was really for my husband and our son. It was all very helpful, and we made it." The man went back to school to prepare for a new career. And when the son saw dad returning to school, he studied harder.

Counselors have found that the couples who make it through job-loss crises are usually the ones in which the "strong" spouse—the one whose self-esteem is still intact—seek out what is *best* for the wounded spouse. If your spouse has been wounded in some way, think about what you can do to show that you will genuinely believe in your spouse's goodness.

*Love bears all things, believes all things,*
*hopes all things, endures all things.*
I CORINTHIANS 13:7 RSV

In *The Hungering Dark,* Frederick Buechner writes eloquently: "The reality of the bride and groom, which is also their joy, is of course that they love each other; but whereas sentimentality tends to stop right there and have a good cry, candor has to move on with eyes at least dry enough to see through. They love each other indeed, and in a grim world their love is a delight to behold, but love as a response of the heart to loveliness, love as primarily an emotion, is only part of what a Christian wedding celebrates, and beyond it are levels that sentimentality cannot see. Because the promises that are given are not just promises to love the other when the other is lovely and lovable, but to love the other for better

*Marriage takes commitment; all good things do.*

or for worse, for richer or for poorer, in sickness and in health, and that means to love the other even at half-past three in the morning when the baby is crying and to love each other with a terrible cold in the head and when the bills have to be paid. The love that is affirmed at a wedding is not just a condition of the heart but an act of the will, and the promise that love makes is to will the other's good even at the expense sometimes of its own good—and that is quite a promise."

*So guard yourself in your spirit, and do not break faith with the wife of your youth.*
MALACHI 2:15 NIV

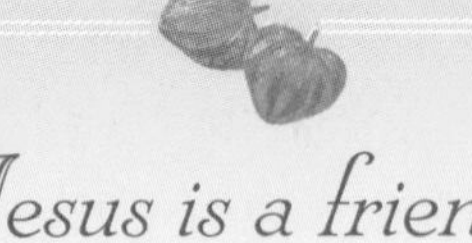

*Jesus is a friend who walks in when the world has walked out.*

Babe Ruth hit 714 home runs during his baseball career, but on this particular day toward the end of his career, the Braves were playing the Reds in Cincinnati, and the great Bambino was no hero. He fumbled the ball and threw badly. In one inning alone, his errors were responsible for most of the five runs scored by Cincinnati.

As the Babe walked off the field and headed toward the dugout after the third out, a crescendo of angry cries and boos rose to greet him. Then . . . a boy jumped over the railing and ran out onto the field. With tears streaming down his face, he threw his arms around the legs of his hero.

Ruth didn't hesitate for a second. He picked up the boy, hugged him, then set him down and patted his head. The cries from the crowd abruptly stopped. A hush fell over the entire park. In that brief moment, the fans saw two heroes on the field: Ruth, who, in spite of his own dismal day in fielding, cared about the feelings of a young fan; and a small boy, who cared about the feelings of another human being.

No matter your performance on the playing field of life today, the Lord has a hug awaiting you at the day's end. He is your Number One Fan.

*These things I have spoken unto you, that in me ye might have peace. In the world ye shall have tribulation: but be of good cheer; I have overcome the world.*

JOHN 16:33

A new wife nagged her husband about not overeating and losing ten pounds. When she finally realized her nagging wasn't motivating him, but rather was hurting him, because he didn't feel accepted by her, she changed her tactics. She began to prepare low-fat meals, with only two servings. She never brought home junk food. And she encouraged her husband to join a gym with his friends. The result was that her husband lost weight and maintained his weight loss.

*When Adam was lonely, God created for him not ten friends, but one wife.*

This same woman also gave careful thought to her husband's education. He had worked full-time during his college years and thus hadn't finished his degree. When he was considering a potential job change, he felt that he wasn't very marketable. So she helped him research degree programs designed for working people. Then once he decided on a program, she brainstormed ideas with him, helped with library research, quizzed him at test time, and typed his papers. He graduated with honors.

Was this woman trying to "make" her husband into something he wasn't? "No," she insists. "These were things my husband both wanted and was capable of doing. We were building a future together. What I did to help *him* ultimately helped *us.*"

*A wife of noble character who can find?*
*She is worth far more than rubies.*
PROVERBS 31:10 NIV

# *"Family" was God's idea, and He does not make mistakes.*

An old minister once said, "A couple that tries to build a good marriage without God's Word is like someone trying to sit on a three-legged stool that has one leg missing."

The couple who depends on Scripture for solutions to problems they encounter has a distinct advantage over the family with no faith. The Bible is a "window," of sorts, into the mind of the Heavenly Father. It tells us how and why the Creator established marriage and the family and gives us all the principles necessary for a long, lasting, and loving relationship with another person—with very practical advice on everything from sexual attitudes, to handling money, to disciplining children. The Bible is the ultimate "Handbook on Marriage."

It's not enough, however, for a couple to merely read Scripture. They must also pray and ask God for the wisdom and courage to *apply* the truth that they read to their lives. They must live out God's Word in their daily activities—in all they say and do. Only then can the Bible have real meaning and impact upon their marriage.

Perhaps the greatest treasure any family can ever have is a well-worn family Bible.

*For this cause a man shall leave his father and his mother, and shall cleave to his wife; and they shall become one flesh.*

GENESIS 2:24 NAS

"If I can throw a single ray of light across the darkened pathway of another; if I can aid some soul to clearer sight of life and duty, and thus bless my brother; if I can wipe from any human cheek a tear, I shall not have lived my life in vain while here.

*The measure of a man's character is not what he gets from his ancestors, but what he leaves his descendants.*

"If I can guide some erring one to truth, inspire within his heart a sense of duty; if I can plant within my soul of rosy youth a sense of right, a love of truth and beauty; if I can teach one man that God and heaven are near, I shall not have lived in vain while here.

"If from my mind I banish doubt and fear, and keep my life attuned to love and kindness; if I can scatter light and hope and cheer, and help remove the curse of mental blindness; if I can make more joy, more hope, less pain, I shall not have lived and loved in vain.

"If by life's roadside I can plant a tree, beneath whose shade some wearied head may rest, though I may never share its beauty, I shall yet be truly blest—though no one knows my name, nor drops a flower upon my grave, I shall not have lived in vain while here."—*Anonymous*

*A good man leaveth an inheritance to his children's children: and the wealth of the sinner is laid up for the just.*
PROVERBS 13:22

*The best way to get the last word is to apologize.*

A woman in a fancy luxury car waited patiently in a crowded mall lot for a parking place to open up. She drove up and down between the rows until finally she saw a man with a load of packages head for his car. She followed him and parked behind him, waiting while he opened his trunk and loaded it. Finally he got into his car and backed out. Just as she was preparing to pull forward into the space, a young man in a little sports car—coming from the opposite direction—turned in front of her, zipped into the space, got out of his car, and started walking away. The woman was livid. She shouted from her big luxury car, "Hey, young man! I was waiting for that parking place."

The teenager responded, "Sorry, lady, but that's how it is when you're young and quick." She instantly put her car into gear, floorboarded it, and crashed into the sports car, crushing its right rear fender. Now it was the young man's turn to jump up and down, shouting, "What are you doing?" The woman in the luxury car calmly responded, "Well, son, that's how it is when you're old and rich."

Most of the world's problems and conflicts could probably be resolved if, instead of retaliation and revenge, apologies were made all around.

*If you have been trapped by what you said,*
*ensnared by the words of your mouth,*
*then do this, my son, to free yourself, since*
*you have fallen into your neighbor's*
*hands: Go and humble yourself;*
*press your plea with your neighbor!*
PROVERBS 6:2,3 (NIV)

Virginia Satir was once quoted in a *Reader's Digest* article as giving this advice for the cure of the blues: "Our pores are places for messages of love and physical contact. . . . Four hugs a day are necessary for survival, eight for maintenance, and twelve for growth."

*Hug therapy really works.*

How many people do you know who might benefit from taking that prescription? If those people are in your own family or circle of friends, you can be part of their emotional health and growth!

Scientists have long recognized that our skin is the most extensive organ of the human body. Our skin is designed to receive sensation. Every minute section is filled with nerve endings that are quick to respond to changes in temperature, pressure, and light.

It is through the sense of touch that we come to know friend from foe. It is through touch that the deepest and most endearing expressions of love are made. It is through touch that we communicate messages that lie beyond our ability to use words.

*Reach out and touch someone today* is good advice on many levels!

*Love one another with brotherly affection, giving precedence* and *showing honor to one another.*
ROMANS 12:10 AMP

# Acknowledgements

We acknowledge and thank the following people for the quotes used in this book: Joseph and Lois Bird (12), James Dobson (14,40,43,109,170,270,274,294), C. S. Lewis (15), William Raspberry (17), Colleen and Louis Evans, Jr. (19,127), Shirley Boone (21), James H. Jauncey (27), H. Norman Wright (30), Mother Teresa (32), Joseph Joubert (36), Dan Bennett (38), Charles W. Shedd (39,63,157), Margaret Fuller (46), Erma Bombeck (47), Mae West (48), Charles Meigs (52), Leonard E. LeSourd (53), Richard Dobbins (54), Ken Anderson (57), Colleen Evans (61,229), Don Osgood (65), Margaret E. Sanger (66), Thomas a'Kempis (68), George MacDonald (69), Martin Luther (70,93,99), Alvin Vander Griend (72), Bill and Lynne Hybels (73,115), Ruth Bell Graham (74,285), Matthew and Dennis Linn (77), George Adams (78), Paul McElroy (81,243), Winston Churchill (82), Walter Hines Page (87), Glen Wheeler (88), President Dwight Eisenhower (89), Ogden Nash (92), Marie Louise De La Ramee (93), Robert and Rosemary Barnes (95,119), Grit (96), Renee Jordan (104), Abigail Van Buren (105), Ron Mehl (107), Lady Bird Johnson (108), Joanne Caufman (113), Walter Trobisch (121), Mignon McLaughlin (122), Wilfred A. Peterson (124,276), Bishop Jeremy Taylor (126), Francis Bacon (127), Franklin P. Jones (130), Edith Shaeffer (131,149), Mike Mason (133,139,167,223), Lucretius (134), Jerry Adler (137), Katherine Ann Porter (142), Ignacy Paderewski (144),

Stan Mooneyham (145), Heine (146), Henry W. Longfellow (152,292), Andre Maurois (154), Louis Fromm (158), Marabel Morgan (159), James Thurber (160), Hazel Scot (164), Joni Eareckson Tada (165), Maria Lovell (166), George Eliot (172), R. A. Heinlein (178), Robert Fulghum (179), Marion Stroud (181), Dennis Rainey (188), Peter Devries (190), Samuel Rogers (192), Gordon MacDonald (193), David Ingles (194), Patricia Sprinkle (197), Robert W. Burns (198), Lewis Smedes (199), Ann Landers (201), Richard Exley (205), Howard and Jeanne Hendricks (214), Jerry McCant (222), Joseph Addison (228), G. K. Chesterton (230), St. Francis of Assisi (231), Doris Day (232), Anita Baker (233), Mary Kay Ash (236,280), Konrad Adenauer (238), Thomas Fuller (240), Neil Warren (244), Benjamin Franklin (248), Paul E. Tsongas (250), Anne Morrow Lindberg (253), John D. MacDonald (262), Peter Marshall (264), Betty Mills (266), Thomas A. Edison (273), Norman Wright (281), Kin Hubbard (282), Balzac (284), Michael Green (288), C. A. Lufburrow (291), Ann Wells (295), Harold S. Hulbert (296), M. Shain (298), Frederick Buechner (307), Virginia Satir (309).